The Butterfly Book

The Butterfly Book

A Reading and Writing Course

Irina Tyk

Civitas: Institute for the Study of Civil Society
London

Registered Charity No. 1085494

First Published 2007

Text © Irina Tyk 2007

Illustrations and layout © Civitas 2007

Published by
Civitas
77 Great Peter Street
London SW1P 2EZ

Civitas is a registered charity (no. 1085494)
and a company limited by guarantee, registered in
England and Wales (no. 04023541)

email: books@civitas.org.uk

ISBN 978-1-903386-61-3

Independence: The Institute for the Study of Civil Society (Civitas) is a registered educational charity (No. 1085494) and a company limited by guarantee (No. 04023541). Civitas is financed from a variety of private sources to avoid over-reliance on any single or small group of donors.

All publications are independently refereed. All the Institute's publications seek to further its objective of promoting the advancement of learning. The views expressed are those of the authors, not of the Institute.

Designed and typeset by Richard Kelly
Illustrations by Ed Dovey

Printed in Great Britain by
The Cromwell Press Group, Trowbridge

Contents

The Adventures of Ponti Panda

About the author

Irina Tyk is an honours graduate of the University of London. She has lectured at the University of Wales and the University of St. Andrews. Presently she is the Headmistress of Holland House School, an independent preparatory school.

She believes in the intellectual development of very young children in the structured environment of whole-class teaching. She believes that after one year at school children should be able to read independently. She continues to present these views on television and in public debate.

Irina Tyk is a director of The Butterfly Project, set up in 1991, and of Butterfly Educational Enterprises, set up in 2005, to run summer courses for children who wish to benefit from a rational and purposeful teaching approach.

Introduction

In 1989 I became Head of a school for children aged 4 to 11, and so in an instant I assumed overall responsibility for turning young non-readers into young readers. My first step was to look at the many existing reading schemes. It was at that moment that I received something of a shock to discover that children in England were taught to read by a method that largely ignored the fact that the letters of the alphabet are symbols that denote sounds. Consequently, learning to read at that time had become something of a hit and miss approach that relied on the memorisation of whole words and the application of contextual cues often in the form of pictures. Such reading strategies reflected the widespread opinion that the English language contained too many exceptions and too many spelling anomalies to be taught in a coherent and systematic fashion. The exceptions had overwhelmed the consistencies!

As often occurs when the heavy hand of orthodoxy is in the ascendant, the dissidents are forced to disseminate material via a kind of underground network. And so I found myself among a small number of like-minded teachers and educationalists who continued to teach children to read as our grandparents and great-grandparents had once been taught. Long before modern theoreticians rethought the matter, there was neither mystery nor enigma in how children were taught to read at their mother's knee or in their first year at school.

In 1991 I founded the Butterfly Reading Project which brought me out of the Head's office and into the classroom. With a number of colleagues, I ran classes in the summer vacation for children who for some reason or other had failed to learn to read. I have seen rows and rows of young faces, hesitant and fearful of the squiggles on the page, and I have seen these same young children freed by the discovery that learning to read is not nearly as hard as it first seemed.

It is not an uncommon psychological trait that those who find themselves in disagreement with the establishment soon find themselves in disagreement with fellow-travellers too. I am not an exception to this principle and soon enough I felt the need to present my own version of how children should be taught to read in the classroom, at home or anywhere else where one person has the responsibility to teach another to read. And so The Butterfly Book was born. It is how we teach children to read at Holland House School; it is how many children learn to read at other schools and it has been used most successfully at a number of reading courses set up specifically to improve reading standards.

Above all, I am a teacher; I wrote The Butterfly Book so that children may be taught to read easily, quickly and with a lot of pleasure.

Irina Tyk
Holland House School
July 2007

First Principles

- There are only 44 sounds in the English language. Once these sounds have been learned and *blended* to form words then the task of learning to read is complete.

- The best way to teach children to read lies in paying close attention to blending sounds. Consequently it is essential that children *blend* sounds from the very beginning of the course.

- This is not a workbook, and so all written exercises should be completed in a separate exercise book. Filling in the gaps on the page is counter-productive. In each case, the whole word should be written out so that the principle of blending is further re-enforced.

- This reading course is consistent with the belief that it is the proper concern of education to discover and reveal integrating principles rather than present information arbitrarily. This course teaches children to read by reference to fixed rules and guidelines which can be applied to most of the language. Those well-documented and familiar English words which defy normal sound patterns are treated as exceptions which do not lie at the core of learning to read proficiently and independently.

- For the majority of children, learning to read will be their first experience of formal education. It is imperative that this first learning model demonstrate to the young pupil that knowledge is knowable by reference to integrating principles. This reading course enables pupils to learn how to read thousands of words without having to memorise the words themselves.

- Each chapter in this book introduces a new sound. The letters which denote the sound should be learned as they appear in the course. It is not necessary in order to learn to read to memorise a particular fixed sequence of letters as set out in the alphabet.

- At the beginning of the course it may be useful to place a ruler under each line of text, so that the student is encouraged to focus more effectively and to acquire the habit of reading from left to right.

- One learns the alphabet by memorising the names of the letters in a specific order; one learns to read by decoding the sounds of the letters. When using this book, children must always refer to letters and letter-combinations by their sounds and not by the names of the letters.

- Learning to read and write should be taught simultaneously from the very beginning. Children should be encouraged to write on lines from the start.

- Intentionally, there are no pictures in this reading course so that children can learn to read without external prompts and cues.

Some Guidelines on Handwriting

- Letters must sit on the line. Children should write on lines from the very beginning.

- Letters must be of reasonable size – in proportion to the space between the lines.

- There must be a reasonable and consistent gap between words.

- Children should sit with correct posture. Strange physical contortions must be corrected. The non-writing hand must hold the book and not be allowed to dangle freely. The writing implement should be held properly.

- Joined-up writing should be introduced as the first writing skill. Children may read print but they should not write in print. A facilitating curve should be regarded as part of the letter and not something that is added later.

- Children should write with a thick soft-leaded pencil which is properly sharpened. The transition to pen should follow later.

- Handwriting is not an artistic skill. It is not calligraphy. Beautifully formed archaic constructions are best left in an aesthetic environment. **Handwriting is a practical skill which is all about clarity, speed and legibility!**

- Different children will develop different writing styles. There is nothing wrong with this so long as the above rules are observed.

Key to Lessons

	VOWEL SOUNDS	KEY WORDS	CONSONANT SOUNDS	KEY WORDS	Page
LESSON 1	a	(as in fat)	t n	(as in tan)	19
LESSON 2			P	(as in nap)	21
LESSON 3			d m	(as in mad)	23
LESSON 4			l	(as in lap)	25
LESSON 5			b	(as in tab)	28
LESSON 6			h	(as in hat)	31
LESSON 7			f	(as in fan)	33
LESSON 8			g	(as in gag)	35
LESSON 9			s ss	(as in sat & mass)	37
LESSON 10	i	(as in pin)			39
LESSON 11			r	(as in rat)	44
LESSON 12			z	(as in is)	47
LESSON 13	A I	(as in At & It)			49
LESSON 14			T N P	(as in Tim, Nat & Pip)	51
LESSON 15			D M L	(as in Dan, Mat & Lift)	52
LESSON 16			B H F	(as in Bat, Hat & Fat)	53

Key to Lessons *(continued)*

	VOWEL SOUNDS	KEY WORDS	CONSONANT SOUNDS	KEY WORDS	Page
LESSON 33	ee ea	(as in bee & tea)			94
LESSON 34	e	(as in me)			98
LESSON 35	ay ai	(as in say & sail)			102
LESSON 36	ie igh	(as in tie & sigh)			105
LESSON 37	i l	(as in mild)			108
LESSON 38	oa ow	(as in goat & glow)			110
LESSON 39	a + silent e	(as in fate)			113
LESSON 40	i + silent e	(as in fine)			117
LESSON 41	o + silent e	(as in note)			120
LESSON 42	u + silent e	(as in cute)			123
LESSON 43			wh	(as in when)	125
LESSON 44	oo	(as in moon)			127
LESSON 45	ew ue	(as in grew & blue)			130
LESSON 46	oo	(as in book)			132
LESSON 47	er ir ur	(as in herd, bird & turn)			134

	VOWEL SOUNDS	KEY WORDS	CONSONANT SOUNDS	KEY WORDS	Page
LESSON 48	**er or a**	(as in sister, doctor & China)			**136**
LESSON 49	**oi oy**	(as in toil & boy)			**139**
LESSON 50	**a**	(as in car & bath)			**141**
LESSON 51	**o al aw**	(as in for, talk & law)			**143**
LESSON 52			**ed**	(as in noted)	**146**
LESSON 53			**le**	(as in able)	**148**
LESSON 54			**c**	(as in ace)	**149**
LESSON 55			**g**	(as in gem)	**151**
LESSON 56	**ou ow**	(as in round & cow)			**153**
LESSON 57			**tion sion**	(as in nation & pension)	**156**
LESSON 58			**zh ch**	(as in pleasure & picture)	**158**
LESSON 59			**Ph**	(as in phonics)	**160**
LESSON 60			**some silent letters**	(as in knee, wrong, lamb & school)	**162**
LESSON 61			**qu Q**	(as in quest)	**164**
LESSON 62			**z Z**	(as in zoo)	**165**

❤ LESSON **ONE** ❤

Introduce the short **a** sound (as in **fat**) and the single letter consonant sounds **t** and **n**. It is important to *blend* the sounds made by the vowel and the consonant.

[Note: the much shorter vowel sound of the indefinite article (as in **a** hat) ☞ see **Lesson 26**.]

1. **Read, write and practise:**

a	a	a
t	t	t
n	n	n
ta	ta	ta
at	at	at
na	na	na
an	an	an
tan	tan	tan
ant	ant	ant
nan	nan	nan
tat	tat	tat
an	an	an

2.   Read the following letter sounds and *blend*:

a + t → at

a + n → an

a + n + t → ant

n + a + n → nan

t + a + n → tan

3.   Add a to the following and practise:

...t	...t	...t
...n	...n	...n
...nt	...nt	...nt
t...n	t...n	t...n
n...n	n...n	n...n

Revise the short vowel sound **a** and the single letter consonant sounds **t** and **n**. Introduce the single letter consonant sound **p** and *blend* with the short vowel sound **a**.

1. **Read, write and practise:**

p	p	p
ta	ta	ta
at	at	at
an	an	an
nan	nan	nan
p	p	p
pa	pa	pa
ap	ap	ap
pap	pap	pap
nap	nap	nap
tap	tap	tap
pat	pat	pat
pan	pan	pan
apt	apt	apt
ant	ant	ant
pant	pant	pant

2. **Read the following letter sounds and *blend*:**

$$t + a + p \rightarrow \textbf{tap}$$
$$t + a + n \rightarrow \textbf{tan}$$
$$p + a + t \rightarrow \textbf{pat}$$
$$n + a + p \rightarrow \textbf{nap}$$
$$n + a + n \rightarrow \textbf{nan}$$
$$a + n \rightarrow \textbf{an}$$
$$a + n + t \rightarrow \textbf{ant}$$
$$p + a \rightarrow \textbf{pa}$$
$$p + a + n \rightarrow \textbf{pan}$$
$$p + a + n + t \rightarrow \textbf{pant}$$

3. **Add a to the following and practise:**

n__n	p__t	p__n
n__p	t__p	n__p
t__n	p__t	p__nt

❦ LESSON **THREE** ❦

Revise the short vowel sound **a** and the single letter consonant sounds **t**, **n** and **p**. Introduce the single letter consonant sounds **d** and **m** and *blend* with the short vowel sound **a**.

1. **Read, write and practise:**

d	d	d
m	m	m
t	t	t
n	n	n
p	p	p
d	d	d
da	da	da
ma	ma	ma
ta	ta	ta
na	na	na
pa	pa	pa
pat	pat	pat
tap	tap	tap
ad	ad	ad
am	am	am
mad	mad	mad
mat	mat	mat
dad	dad	dad
pad	pad	pad

2. **Read the following letter sounds and** *blend*:

a + n → an

a + n + t → ant

p + a → pa

p + a + n → pan

p+a+n+t → pant

d + a + d → dad

p + a + d → pad

m + a + d → mad

m + a + t → mat

m + a + n → man

m + a + p → map

a + n → an

a + n + d → and

a + n + t → ant

3. **Add a to the following and practise:**

....m   m....t   m....n

m....p   m....d   d....d

p....d   ....nd   ....nt

❧ LESSON **FOUR** ❧

Revise the short vowel sound **a** and the single letter consonant sounds **t**, **n**, **p**, **d** and **m**. Introduce the single letter consonant sound **l** and *blend* with the short vowel sound **a**.

1. **Read, write and practise:**

l	l	l
t	t	t
n	n	n
p	p	p
d	d	d
m	m	m
l	l	l
la	la	la
ta	ta	ta
na	na	na
pa	pa	pa
da	da	da
ma	ma	ma
lad	lad	lad
lap	lap	lap
al	al	al
pal	pal	pal

2. Read the following letter sounds and *blend*:

a + n → an
a + n + d → and
a + n + t → ant
d + a + d → dad
m + a + d → mad
l + a + d → lad
l + a + p → lap
p + a + l → pal
a + n → an
a + n + t → ant
p+a+n+t → pant
l + a → la
l + a + n → lan
l + a + n + d → land
l + a + m + p → lamp

3. Add **a** to the following and practise:

l..d	l..p	p..l
..nd	l..nd	..m
l..mp	d..mp	p..nt

4. **Revise:**

a	t	n
p	d	m
l		

at	am	an

tap	map	lap
dad	mad	lad
man	nan	pan
pal	tan	nap
and	ant	

pant	lamp	land
damp		

❧ LESSON **FIVE** ❧

Revise the short vowel sound **a** and the single letter consonant sounds **t, n, p, d, m** and **l**. Introduce the single letter consonant sound **b** and *blend* with the short vowel sound **a**.

1. **Read, write and practise:**

b	b	b
t	t	t
n	n	n
p	p	p
d	d	d
m	m	m
l	l	l
b	b	b
ba	ba	ba
ta	ta	ta
pa	pa	pa
da	da	da
ma	ma	ma
la	la	la
bat	bat	bat
ban	ban	ban
bap	bap	bap
bad	bad	bad
ab	ab	ab

tab	tab	tab
dab	dab	dab
lab	lab	lab

2. Read the following letter sounds and *blend*:

a + n → an
a + n + d → and
a + n + t → ant
b + a + t → bat
b + a + n → ban
b + a + p → bap
b + a + d → bad
d + a + b → dab
l + a + b → lab
p+a+n+t → pant
b+a+n+d → band

3. Add **a** to the following and practise:

....n	....nd	b....nd
b....t	b....n	b....p
b....d	l....d	d....d
l....b	l....mp	l....nd

4. **Add t to the following and practise:**

>   **a**......   **ma**......
>
>   **pa**......   **ba**......

5. **Add n to the following and practise:**

>   **a**......   **na**......
>
>   **pa**......   **ma**......
>
>   **ba**......

6. **Add p to the following and practise:**

>   **ta**......   **na**......
>
>   **ma**......   **la**......
>
>   **ba**......   **lam**......
>
>   **dam**......

7. **Add d to the following and practise:**

>   **da**......   **pa**......
>
>   **ma**......   **la**......
>
>   **ba**......

❧ LESSON **SIX** ❧

Revise the short vowel sound **a** and the single letter consonant sounds **t, n, p, d, m, l** and **b**. Introduce the single letter consonant sound **h** and *blend* with the short vowel sound **a**.

1. **Read, write and practise:**

h	h	h
t	t	t
n	n	n
p	p	p
d	d	d
m	m	m
l	l	l
b	b	b
h	h	h
ha	ha	ha
hat	hat	hat
ham	ham	ham
had	had	had
tab	tab	tab
lab	lab	lab
ban	ban	ban
dad	dad	dad
bat	bat	bat
hat	ham	had

2. **Read the following letter sounds and *blend*:**

a + n → an
a + n + d → and
a + n + t → ant
h + a + t → hat
h + a + m → ham
h + a + d → had
p + a + n + t → pant
b + a + n + d → band
l + a + n + d → land
h + a + n + d → hand

3. **Add a to the following and practise:**

h␣t	h␣m	h␣d
␣n	␣t	␣m
l␣nd	b␣nd	h␣nd
b␣t	p␣nt	l␣mp

Revise the short vowel sound **a** and the single letter consonant sounds **t, n, p, d, m, l, b** and **h**. Introduce the single letter consonant sound **f** and *blend* with the short vowel sound **a**.

[Note the phonic exception: **o** + **f** ☞ **of** (as in **Ovid**).]

1. **Read, write and practise:**

f	f	f
t	t	t
n	n	n
p	p	p
d	d	d
m	m	m
l	l	l
b	b	b
h	h	h
f	f	f
fa	fa	fa
fat	fat	fat
fan	fan	fan
fad	fad	fad

2. **Read the following letter sounds and *blend*:**

> **a + n + d → and**
> **b + a + n +d → band**
> **l + a + n + d → land**
> **h + a + n + d → hand**
> **f + a + n → fan**
> **f + a + t → fat**

3. **Now try these:**

> **fan → flan**
> **fat → flat**
> **fab → flab**
> **pan → plan**
> **ban → band → bland**

4. **Add a to the following and practise:**

> **___n**   **f___n**
> **___t**   **f___t**
> **fl___n**   **fl___t**
> **fl___b**   **pl___n**
> **bl___nd**

Revise the short vowel sound **a** and the single letter consonant sounds **t, n, p, d, m, l, b, h**, and **f**. Introduce the single letter consonant sound **g** (as in **gag**) and *blend* with the short vowel sound **a**.

1. **Read, write and practise**

g	g	g
t	n	p
d	m	l
b	h	f
g	g	g
ga	ga	ga
gap	gap	gap
gab	gab	gab
ag	ag	ag
tag	tag	tag
nag	nag	nag
mag	mag	mag
bag	bag	bag
gag	gag	gag

2. **Read the following letter sounds and *blend*:**

> g + a + p → gap
> g + a + b → gab
> t + a + g → tag
> n + a + g → nag
> m + a + g → mag
> b + a + g → bag
> g + a + g → gag

3. **Now try these:**

> fan → flan
> fat → flat
> fab → flab
> lag → flag
> lad → glad
> ban → band → bland

4. **Add a to the following and practise:**

> g.....g   g.....p   m.....g
> t.....g   l.....g   n.....g
> b.....g   fl.....g   gl.....d

5. **Add g to the following and practise:**

> la.....   na.....   ba.....
> ta.....   fla.....   .....lad

❧ LESSON **NINE** ❧

Revise the short vowel sound **a** and the single letter consonant sounds **t, n, p, d, m, l, b, h, f** and **g**. Introduce the single letter consonant sound **s** (as in **sat**) and the double letter consonant sound **ss** (as in **mass**) and *blend* with the short vowel sound **a**.

1. **Read, write and practise:**

s	s	s
sa	sa	sa
sat	sat	sat
sap	sap	sap
sad	sad	sad
sand	sand	sand
mass	mass	mass
lass	lass	lass

2. **Read the following letter sounds and *blend*:**

s + a + t → sat
s + a + p → sap
s + a + d → sad
s + a + n + d → sand
m + a + ss → mass
l + a + ss → lass

3. Now try these:

> lab → slab
> nag → snag
> tag → stag
> tab → stab
> lap → slap → slaps
> nap → snap → snaps
> and → sand → stand

4. Add **a** to the following and practise:

s....t   s....p   s....d
st....nd   m....ss   l....ss

5. Add **s** to the following practise:

ant....   hat....   map....
tap....   lamp....   pant....
....tab   ....tag   ....nag
....lap   ....lam   ....lab

✿ LESSON **TEN** ✿

Introduce the short vowel sound **i** (as in **pin**) and *blend* with the single letter consonant sounds **t, n, p, d, m, l, b, h, f, g** and **s.**

1. Read, write and practise:

i	i	i
it	it	it
in	in	in
if	if	if
ti	ti	ti
ni	ni	ni
tin	tin	tin
pin	pin	pin
din	din	din
nip	nip	nip
dim	dim	dim
mid	mid	mid
lid	lid	lid
fig	fig	fig
big	big	big
dig	dig	dig
pig	pig	pig
him	him	him
bin	bin	bin
nib	nib	nib

nil	nil	nil
did	did	did
gig	gig	gig
bib	bib	bib
sit	sit	sit
sits	sits	sits
sip	sip	sip
sips	sips	sips
pip	pip	pip
pips	pips	pips
hip	hip	hip
hips	hips	hips
fit	fit	fit
fits	fits	fits
tip	tip	tip
tips	tips	tips
pit	pit	pit
pits	pits	pits
imp	imp	imp
imps	imps	imps

2. **Read the following letter sounds and *blend*:**

i + n → in
i + t → it
s + i + t → sit
d + i + d → did
p + i + p → pip
g + i + g → gig
b + i + g → big
s + l + i + m → slim
l + i + s + t → list
m + i + s + t → mist
f + i + s + t → fist

3. **Now try these:**

lit → slit → slits
lip → slip → slips
lip → blip → blips
sit → spit → spits

lip → lips → lisps
lip → limp → limpid
lint → splint → splints

4. **Add i to the following and practise:**

...n	...t	...f
...mp	p...n	d...n
t...n	t...p	l...d
d...d	l...p	l...t
sl...p	sl...d	bl...p
l...st	m...st	f...st

t...m...d   l...mp...d   l...m...t

5. **Add n to the following and practise:**

ti...	pi...	di...
bi...	si...	fi...

6. **Add p to the following and practise:**

ti...	hi...	li...
si...	di...	ni...

7. **Add g to the following and practise:**

pi...	di...	bi...
fi...	gi...	...ift

8. **Add s to the following and practise:**

tip...	lip...	sit...
bit...	hit...	pit...

9. **Revise a (as in pan) and i (as in pin):**

an	in
at	it
tan	tin
tap	tip
pat	pit
pan	pin
dad	did
mad	mid
lad	lid
lab	lib
lap	lip
bat	bit
ban	bin
bag	big
hat	hit
ham	him
had	hid
fan	fin
fat	fit
sat	sit
mass	miss
slam	slim
slap	slip
span	spin

❧ LESSON **ELEVEN** ❧

Introduce the single letter consonant sound **r** and *blend* with the short vowel sounds **a** and **i**.

1. **Read, write and practise:**

r	r	r
ra	ra	ra
ran	ran	ran
rat	rat	rat
rag	rag	rag
ri	ri	ri
rig	rig	rig
rid	rid	rid
rim	rim	rim
rip	rip	rip
rib	rib	rib
rift	rift	rift
rand	rand	rand
tram	tram	tram
trap	trap	trap
trim	trim	trim
trip	trip	trip
gram	gram	gram
grab	grab	grab
gran	gran	gran

grand	grand	grand
grid	grid	grid
grim	grim	grim
grit	grit	grit
grin	grin	grin

2. **Read the following letter sounds and *blend*:**

r + a + n → ran
r + a + t → rat
r + i + m → rim
r + i + b → rib
g + r + a + n → gran
g + r + i + n → grin

3. **Now try these:**

rap → trap → strap
rip → trip → strip
ran → gran → grand

4. **Add a to the following and practise:**

r__n	r__t	r__g
r__nd	gr__n	gr__nd
tr__p	tr__m	str__p

5. **Add i to the following and practise:**

r___m   r___b   r___g
r___d   gr___n   gr___m
gr___t   tr___p   tr___m

6. **See how you can make different words by adding a
    or i to the following:**

gr___n   gr___n
tr___m   tr___m
pr___m   pr___m
str___p   str___p
sp___ns   sp___ns
m___ss   m___ss
gr___m   gr___m
fl___t   fl___t

❧ LESSON **TWELVE** ❧

Introduce the single letter consonant sound **s** (as in **is**) and the single letter consonant sound **s** (as in **dads**).

[Rule: when **s** is used to form a plural it sounds like **z** except after **f**, **k**, **p** and **t**.]

1. **Read, write and practise:**

as	is
has	his
tans	tins
pans	pins
lads	lids
bans	bins
fans	fins
rams	rims
slams	slims
spans	spins

2. **Read the following letter sounds and** *blend*:

a + s → as
h + a + s → has
i + s → is
h + i + s → his
f + a + n + s → fans
f + i + n + s → fins

s + p + a + n + s → **spans**
s + p + i + n + s → **spins**
l + a + m + p + s → **lamps**
l + i + m + p + s → **limps**
s + l + a + p + s → **slaps**
s + l + i + p + s → **slips**
f + l + a + p + s → **flaps**
f + l + i + p + s → **flips**

3. **Add s to make plurals:**

pan.....	**pin**.....
fan.....	**fin**.....
lad.....	**lid**.....
rag.....	**rig**.....
ram.....	**rim**.....
tan.....	**tin**.....
bat.....	**bit**.....
lad.....	**lid**.....
tap.....	**tip**.....
flat.....	**flit**.....

❦ LESSON **THIRTEEN** ❦

Introduce the capital letter **A** (for the short vowel sound **a** as in **At**) and the capital letter **I** (for the short vowel sound **i** as in **It**).

1. **Read, write and practise:**

a	A
an	An
at	At
in	In
it	It
if	If
is	Is

It is big.   Is it big?
It is fat.   Is it fat?
It is him.   Is it him?
It is grand.   Is it grand?
It is bland.   Is it bland?
It is timid.   Is it timid?

It is an ant.
It is his big hat.
It is his big band.
It is his grand plan.
It is his sad and timid nan.

It has big hands.
It had big hands.
It spins.
It grins at him.

If it is big it is fat.
As it is big it is fat.

An ant is timid.
An imp is bad.

In it is an ant.
If it is his band it is grand.

Is his hand damp? It is.
Is his map in his hand? It is.

1. **Read, write and practise:**

t	T
tan	Tim
n	N
nan	Nat
p	P
pal	Pat
pad	Pam

Tim is as fat as Nat.
Timid nan is sad.
Trim Pam has big hands.
Pat is slim and trim.
Nan is sad and timid.
Pin it in his hat.
Pip is his pal.
In it stands Tim.
An ant sat in his flat tin.
Nat has grand plans and is glad.

1. **Read, write and practise:**

d	D
dad	Dan
m	M
man	Mat
miss	Mab
l	L
lad	Lapland

Man plans.
Mat has grand plans.
Dad films his trips in Lapland.
Lift it in and list it as big.
List it in his plan.
Mat, Mab and Dan sit in his big band.
Timid Tim sits in his flat.

1. **Read, write and practise:**

b	B
big	Batman
h	H
his	His
f	F
fat	Finland

Ban it.
His big pal is Batman.
Fit it in.
Fat nan ran in.
Fat Pam has big hands.
Dad films his trips in Finland.
His Dad grins at his grand plans.

1.   **Read, write and practise:**

g	G
gag	Gran
s	S
sat	Sam
r	R
rat	Rat

Grab his big flat hands.
Sit in.
Sam is in splints.
Rat is fat and fit and big.
Gran sits and spins and is glad.

Bad Rin Tin Tin ran in and bit timid Tim.

Introduce the short vowel sound **o** (as in **pot**) and the capital letter **O** and blend with the single consonant sounds **t**, **n**, **p**, **d**, **m**, **l**, **b**, **h**, **f**, **g**, **s** and **r**.

1. Read write and practise:

o	o	o
on	on	on
not	not	not
pot	pot	pot
dot	dot	dot
lot	lot	lot
hot	hot	hot
got	got	got
rot	rot	rot
top	top	top
pop	pop	pop
mop	mop	mop
hop	hop	hop
dog	dog	dog
log	log	log
fog	fog	fog
don	don	don
nod	nod	nod
pod	pod	pod

sob	sob	sob
bond	bond	bond
pond	pond	pond
soft	soft	soft
loft	loft	loft
moss	moss	moss
loss	loss	loss
toss	toss	toss
O	O	O
On	On	On

2. **Read the following letter sounds and *blend*:**

o + n → on
O + n → On
n + o + t → not
h + o + t → hot
l + o + t → lot
l + o + p → lop

3. **Now try these:**

lot → slot → slots
pot → spot → spots
rot → trot → trots
sob → snob → snobs

4. **Add o to the following and practise:**

_n	n_t	t_p
d_t	g_t	h_t
p_p	pl_p	l_st

5. **Revise a (as in pan), i (as in pin) and o (as in pot):**

a	i	o
an	in	on
hat	hit	hot
tap	tip	top
pat	pit	pot
slap	slip	slop
spat	spit	spot
mass	miss	moss
An	In	On

6. **Read, write and practise:**

Tom is hot.
Ron is not hot.
His hat got lost.
Slap it on.
Robin is not in.
Pin it on his hatband.
Pompom sits on top.
An ant sat on his big hat.

Fat Pam has not got big hands.
It is not hot in Finland.

It is not Ron. It is Dan and his dog.

Rin Tin Tin ran in and did not nip timid Tim.

7. **Add not to the following sentences:**

It is hot. It is .... hot.
It is .... Bob. It is Mat.
His hat is big. His hat is .... big.
Robin is .... in. Robin is in.

Pompom is sad and timid.
Pompom is .... sad and timid.

Ron is on film. Ron is .... on film.
Mab is in Lapland. Mab is .... in Lapland.

**Gran is slim and trim. Gran is ....
slim and trim.**

❧ LESSON **NINETEEN** ❧

Introduce the consonant sound **k** (as in **cat**, **kit** and **sock**) and the capital letters **K** and **C**.

1. **Read write and practise:**

k	k	K
kin	kin	Kin
kit	kit	Kit
kid	kid	Kid
kiss	kiss	Kiss
skid	skid	Skid
skin	skin	Skin
skip	skip	Skip
skim	skim	Skim
ink	ink	Ink
sink	sink	Sink
link	link	Link
blink	blink	Blink
c	c	C
can	can	Can
cat	cat	Cat
cap	cap	Cap
cad	cad	Cad
cab	cab	Cab

cod	cod	**Cod**
cop	cop	**Cop**
cob	cob	**Cob**
tack	tack	**Tack**
pack	pack	**Pack**
back	back	**Back**
sack	sack	**Sack**
rack	rack	**Rack**
black	black	**Black**
flack	flack	**Flack**
slack	slack	**Slack**
track	track	**Track**
tick	tick	**Tick**
pick	pick	**Pick**
lick	lick	**Lick**
sick	sick	**Sick**
stick	stick	**Stick**
dock	dock	**Dock**
mock	mock	**Mock**
lock	lock	**Lock**
sock	sock	**Sock**
rock	rock	**Rock**

2. **Now try these:**

> lick → click → clicks
> lock → clock → clocks
> lock → flock → flocks
> rock → frock → frocks
> mock → smock → smocks
> rack → track → tracks
> lack → slack → slacks

3. **Add k to the following and practise:**

....it	....id	....iss
s....id	s....in	s....ip

4. **Add c to the following and practise:**

....an	....at	....ap
....rag	....rib	....rab

5. **Add ck to the following and practise:**

ta........	ti........	to........
pa........	pi........	po........
sa........	si........	so........
la........	li........	lo........
ra........	Ri........	ro........

6. Read, write and practise:

Nick has socks.

Lock him in.

Pompom is sick.

His black cap is not on.

Pam can kiss Batman.

Robins can sit on rocks.

Dogs can kick cats.

Cats can blink.

Send back his bags.

Can Batman strap it in?

Gran sits back and is not sad.

Slim cats sit on soft socks.

Rin Tin Tin licks his hand.

Can Ron pack it in his sack?

On his back pack is a big black hat.

Dad can film his trips in Lapland and Paris.

Pack his bags and send his pots and pans.

❧ LESSON **TWENTY** ❧

Introduce the single letter consonant sounds **v** and **w** and the capital letters **V** and **W** and *blend* with the short vowel sounds **a**, **i** and **o**.

[Note the phonic exception: **w** + **as** ☞ **was** (as in **because**).]

1. **Read, write and practise:**

v	v	V
va	va	Va
van	van	Van
vat	vat	Vat
livid	livid	Livid
vivid	vivid	Vivid
pavilion	pavilion	Pavilion
w	w	W
wag	wag	Wag
win	win	Win
wit	wit	Wit
wig	wig	Wig
wok	wok	Wok
wink	wink	Wink
wick	wick	Wick
swim	swim	Swim

2. **Add v to the following and practise:**

.....at .....an .....im

li.....id .....i.....id pa.....ilion

3. **Add w to the following and practise:**

.....in .....it .....ig
.....ag .....ink .....ick

4. **Read, write and practise:**

> **Pat it and it wags.**
> **Trim his black wig.**
> **Dad winks at fat Sam.**
> **Bob is not fat and can swim.**
> **Tim is not timid and can win.**
> **In his grand plan Mat wins.**
>
> **Ovid stands on his hands and winks.**

5. **Practise this common word which has a special sound:**

> **was   was   was**
>
> **It is black. It was pink.**
> **Ovid was fat and sad.**
> **Ovid is slim and glad.**
> **Ovid was in films.**

Bob was hot in his hat.

Ink is black. His pen was red.

Timid Bob had pens and clocks in his sack.

Black cats blink and can hiss at dogs.

His dog licks his hand and trots back.

Pat skips in pink pants and claps.

Mat stands in soft, pink socks and pats fat Sam on his black wig.

Red pens and black pens sit in big pots.

His pet dog swims in ponds.

Clocks can stop if it is hot.

Fran was not hot. Dad was.

Sam was not timid. Mat was.

It is pink. It was not pink.

It was not red. It was black.

❧ LESSON **TWENTY-ONE** ❧

Introduce the short vowel sound **e** (as in **ten**) and the capital letter **E** and *blend*.

[Note the spelling irregularities which denote the same short vowel sound: **ea** (as in **head**), **ai** (as in **said**) and **ie** (as in **friend**).]

1. **Read, write and practise:**

e	e	e
ten	net	pet
met	let	bet
get	set	den
men	pen	red
vet	wet	wed
web	end	lend
send	bend	fend
mend	tend	tens
dent	sent	rent
left	neck	fleck
deck	less	mess
blend	trend	spend
stem	stress	Fred
Ted	Ben	Meg
Tess	Ed	Edwin

2. **Add e to the following and practise:**

....nd	p....n	t....n
m....n	g....t	r....d
s....t	n....t	l....t
d....n	p....t	b....t
w....b	w....t	v....t
h....n	s....nt	s....nd
sp....nd	B....n	M....g

3. **Revise a (as in pan), i (as in pin), o (as in pot) and e (as in pet):**

pan	pin	pot	pet
nan	nit	not	net
tan	tin	top	ten
dad	did	don	den
man	mid	mop	men
lap	lip	lot	let
hat	his	hot	hen
gag	gig	got	get
fan	fin	fog	fen
rag	rim	rot	red
sap	sip	sop	set
bat	bit	boss	bet
wag	wig	wok	wed

4. Read, write and practise:

> Ten men hid in his den.
> Meg is as red as Bess.
> His wig is wet.
> Len is as timid as Ted.

5. Here are some common words which sound the same but are spelt differently:

> said   head
> friend meant

6. Now practise these sentences:

> Ted said Bob is in bed.
> His friend has big hands.
> His head is big.
>
> Fred said Edwin was his best friend.
> Pam was livid and meant it.
> If it is hot, his friends swim.
> His friend hit him on the head and was sad.
> His hat was on his head. It was big and black and hid his wig.
> Clocks with big hands stand on his desk.
> His friend said it and meant it.

Revise the double letter consonant sound **ss** (as in **mass**). Introduce the double letter consonant sounds **nn**, **dd**, **gg**, **ll** and **ff**.

[Note: these double letter consonants have the same sound as their single letter equivalents.]

1. **Read, write and practise:**

mass	miss	moss	mess
lass	hiss	loss	less
add	mill	boss	bless
Ann	Bill	cross	cress
gaff	till	floss	stress
crass	fill	gloss	dress
cannot	sill	Ross	press
	hill	doll	Bess
	will	odd	egg
	kill	loll	bell
	frill	toll	tell
	grill	trolls	fell
	still	off	sell
	spill	toff	well
	trill	boffin	spell
	ill	soffit	Nell

2. **Add ll to the following and practise:**

be........	mi........	we........
wi........	do........	te........
fe........	se........	hi........
spi........	tri........	gri........

3. **Read, write and practise:**

Bill is ill.
Ann will fit it in.
Nell will not sell it.
Big Jim will tell Bess.
Tess will miss Ron.
Tell him less.
Moss is wet and damp.
Dan will miss his nan.
Is Ross well?
Fran is not well.

4. **Read and see how many words you can find with double consonants:**

Fat Sam is hot in his pink pants. His dog Pompom skips and trots. Pompom fell and felt ill. Pompom is sick. His leg felt bad. Pompom will not trot and cannot skip. Fat Sam will not yell at him. Fat Sam will not sob as his dog will get well. Pompom licks his hand and drinks milk.

Introduce the two-letter consonant sound **ng** (as in **sang**, **sing**, and **song**) and *blend*.

[Note the spelling rule: there must always be two consonants before **ing** unless the original word ends in a silent **e**.]

1. **Read, write and practise:**

sang	**sing**	**song**
bang	**ring**	**long**
hang	**wing**	**gong**
rang	**fling**	**strong**
fang	**sling**	**prong**
gang	**bring**	
pang	**sting**	
slang	**string**	

2. **Add ing to the following and practise:**

fill	**pant**	**rock** ....
sing	**kiss**	**will** ....
lick	**tell**	**milk** ....
sell	**smell**	**sting** ....

3. Now try these:

map → mapping	miss → missing
fit → fitting	fill → filling
nap → napping	loll → lolling
hit → hitting	hiss → hissing
sit → sitting	sell → selling
sip → sipping	sing → singing
tap → tapping	tell → telling
pin → pinning	spill → spilling
spin → spinning	smell → smelling
hop → hopping	pack → packing
sob → sobbing	sack → sacking
wag → wagging	lick → licking
flap → flapping	back → backing
sag → sagging	kick → kicking
let → letting	rock → rocking
bet → betting	mock → mocking
bat → batting	tick → ticking
fret → fretting	pant → panting
swim → swimming	tint → tinting
pin → pinning	mend → mending
grin → grinning	kiss → kissing
flop → flopping	will → willing
flap → flapping	milk → milking

4. **Read, write and practise:**

Robins sing songs.

Bill is singing songs.

Bess is kissing Tess.

Edwin is selling pink socks.

Gran is packing his black bag.

Let him slip it on.

Ann is winning at ping-pong.

His head is spinning.

Bells ring at weddings.

Frantic Fran is blinking and panicking.

Ovid is swimming in his long pond.

Friends sing songs.

Gran is mending socks.

Ross went on and on and did not stop telling his friends off.

Pink socks and black hats sell well.

❧ LESSON **TWENTY-FOUR** ❧

Introduce the short vowel sound **i** written as **y** at the end of a word (as in **happy**) and the long vowel sound **i** written as **y** at the end of a word (as in **fly**). Practise *blending*.

[Note: the letters **ey** at the end a word sound the same as the letter **y** (as in **happy**) ☞ **donkey** and **monkey**.]

[Rule: the long vowel sound **i** occurs in all one-syllable words ending in **y** preceded by a consonant. In this way the short and long vowel sounds denoted by the letter **y** at the end of a word may be readily identified.]

1.   **Read, write and practise:**

daddy	**silly**	**telly**
hilly	**dolly**	**belly**
baggy	**piggy**	**messy**
holly	**Maggy**	**Tommy**
Sammy	**Sally**	**Mandy**

2.   **Add y to the following and practise:**

tell.....	**sill**.....	**hill**.....
doll.....	**mess**.....	**moss**.....
boss.....	**rock**.....	**wack**.....
sand.....	**hand**.....	**dand**.....
cand.....	**Mand**.....	**Bill**.....

3. **Read, write and practise:**

> **Mandy is mending a dolly.**
> **Tommy is kissing Candy.**
> **Silly Billy is happy.**
> **Daddy is bossy.**
> **Sammy is on telly.**

4. **Read, write and practise:**

fly	**by**	**ply**
my	**sly**	**cry**
sky	**dry**	**try**
fry	**pry**	**spy**

5. **Add y to the following and practise:**

m......	**b**......	**fl**......
sk......	**tr**......	**dr**......
cr......	**fr**......	**sp**......

6. **Read, write and practise:**

> **Bess went by.**
> **Try and bring it in.**
> **My dog is ill.**
> **Bats can fly.**
> **My Nell is sad.**
> **Try and drink it.**

My head is not hot.
My hand is dry.
Sit by him.

7. **Now try these:**

Andy and Sandy can fly.
Timmy is missing his daddy.
Sammy can try candy.
Granny is happy.
Happy Milly can fly.

Maggy is singing pop songs on telly.
My dolly has baggy pink pants on.

Grandad is not as happy as Maggy.
Grandad cannot sing on telly as Maggy can.

Find my socks and bring my baggy hat.

Robins can fly in the sky.

Ann is frying eggs.

My baby is crying.

❧ LESSON **TWENTY-FIVE** ❧

Introduce the consonant sound **y** (as in **yes**) and the capital letter **Y** and *blend*.

[Note: the letter **y** is a semi-vowel – when found at the beginning of a word it behaves like a consonant; otherwise it behaves like a vowel.]

1. **Read, write and practise:**

yap	**yes**
yak	**yen**
yam	**yet**
Yasmin	**yell**

2. **Add y to the following and practise:**

......**es**	......**am**	......**et**
......**ap**	......**ak**	......**en**
......**ell**		

3. **Read, write and practise:**

   Is it pink? Yes.
   Is it black? Yes.
   Is Yasmin singing? Yes.

   Yossi is yelling and Yippy is yapping.

Introduce the indefinite article **a** and the definite article **the**.

[Note: the short vowel sound in the indefinite and definite articles is the same as the **er** sound (as in **sister**) ☞ see **Lesson 48**.]

1. **Read, write and practise:**

a lot	the lot
a pan	the pan
a pin	the pin
a pot	the pot
a pen	the pen
a dolly	the dolly
a lad	the lad
a yen	the yen
a dad	the dad

A wacky bossy Yossi
The wacky bossy Yossi

2. **Add the indefinite article a or A to the following sentences:**

> **It is not ..... dog. It is ..... rabbit.**
> **..... pin is in ..... hat. It is ..... hatpin.**
> **Yasmin is in ..... film.**
>
> **..... red hat is in ..... big bag on ..... mat.**
> **Pompom is not ..... man. Pompom is .....**
> **dog.**

3. **Add the definite article the or The to the following sentences:**

> **Sit still at .... back.**
> **........... dog got wet in .... pond.**
> **........... pen on .... desk is black.**
>
> **Sammy is .... man in .... back hat.**
> **........... damp rag is on .... big mat.**

4. **Now try these:**

> **The rabbit is happy.**
> **It is a happy rabbit.**
>
> **The lamp is on the stand.**
> **It is a big lamp.**
>
> **The wind is strong.**
> **It is a strong wind.**

The hat is on his head.
It is a black hat.

Fat Sam has a pig.
The pig has ten piglets.

A happy man is sitting in a black van.
The man is singing songs.

A film is on the telly.
The man from Finland was a dandy.
The silly fat rat hid from the timid black cat.

A rabbit is soft and fluffy.
The timid rabbit is black.

The film on telly is not a happy film.

The clock on the telly is ticking.

The clock in the shop cost a lot.

A dog can pant. The dog is panting.
A cat can hiss. The cat will hiss at the timid rabbit.

Revise the digraph **th** (as in **the**). Introduce the digraph **th** (as in thin) and *blend*.

1. **Read, write and practise th (as in the):**

the	**than**	**then**
this	**that**	**them**
with		

2. **Read, write and practise th (as in thin):**

thin	**think**	**thank**
thing	**throng**	**Thelma**

3. **Add th to the following and practise:**

........**an**	........**ank**
........**at**	........**ink**
........**is**	........**in**
........**em**	........**ing**
........**en**	........**eft**

4. **Read the following sentences:**

   This is a big pot.
   That is a big pot.

   This lad is not well.
   That lad is not well.

This bell will ring.
That bell will ring.

This is not a timid dog.
That is not a timid dog.

This is black and that is pink.
That is pink and this is black.

Thelma must thank him.
A dog is not a thing.
A man can think.
This fat cat is with that thin man.
This nanny is thrifty. That nanny is not.
Thelma got lost in the throng.

❧ LESSON **TWENTY-EIGHT** ❧

Introduce the digraph **sh** (as in **cash**) and *blend*.

[Note the spelling irregularity ☞ **sugar**.]

1. **Read, write and practise:**

ship	shop	shin
shot	shock	shall
shoddy	shell	shack
sham	shelf	shabby

ash	mash	smash
lash	slash	posh
wish	gash	rash
cash	dash	dish
fish	swish	crash

2. **Add sh to the following and practise:**

.... ock	.... ip	.... in
.... ot	ma	ca ....
di	wi	swi ....

3. Now try these:

Sammy spends cash in the shop.
Andy has a rash on his hand.

This ship cannot dock on dry land.
That shocking pink band sits on a posh black hat.

The tramp in the shabby hat spends his cash on fish and mash.

Introduce the digraph **ch** (as in **chat**) and **tch** (as in **patch**) and *blend*.

1. **Read, write and practise:**

chat	chit	chap
chin	chop	chomp
chill	chimp	check
chip	chilly	rich

match	patch	latch
catch	batch	pitch
ditch	stitch	witch

2. **Add ch to the following and practise:**

ri............ ....in ....op

............ill ....ap pin............

3. **Add tch to the following and practise:**

ma............ pa............ la............

di............ pi............ sti............

4. **Now try these:**

Sit and chat with him.
It is not hot. It is chilly.

His granny is rich.
The lad lit a match.
The witch has a big black hat.
It is pitch black in the pavilion.
Fran can stitch his socks.
Fry fish and chips in a hot pan.

Yasmin is sitting on a bench and chatting with Molly.

It is pitch black.
The witch sits on a patch of damp moss in a ditch.
This rich man is a happy chap.

❧ LESSON **THIRTY** ❧

Introduce the short vowel sound **u** (as in **pun**) and the capital letter **U** and *blend*.

[Note the small number of spelling irregularities which denote the same vowel sound: **one**, **none**, **some**, **come**, and **ough** (as in **enough**), **touch** and **tongue**.]

1. **Read, write and practise:**

u	u	U
tum	nun	pun
fun	sun	mum
run	sum	pup
bun	tut	nut
hum	hut	gut
but	tug	hug
cup	sup	bus
lull	dull	gull
chum	shun	thug
rug	luck	lung
much	such	punch
lunch	brunch	crunch
rush	brush	plum
dust	fuss	fussy

2.   **Add u to the following and practise:**

n....n   f....n   s....n
p....p   n....t   g....t
l....ng   fl....ng   g....ll
pl....m   h....m   st....ng
ch....m   sh....t   l....nch

3.   **Add n to the following and practise:**

ru....   fu....   pu....
gu....   nu....   bu....
su....   shu....   spu....

4.   **Add t to the following and practise:**

nu....   bu....   hu....
gu....   shu....   mus....

5.   **Add m to the following and practise:**

mu....   su....   hu....
tu....   plu....   chu....

6.   **Read the following sentences:**

Gus is sitting in the sun.
His chum hugs his pet pug.

Sit up. Fill up. Run up.
Get up. Set up. Chin up.

Ben will send his chum fresh plums.

Mum will not fuss much if his puppy has fun.

Yasmin will not rush and will miss the bus.

7. **Read:**

On top of a rocky hill sits a fluffy puppy. The puppy runs and frolics happily until a big black cat runs up. The pup huffs and puffs but the cat is not timid. The cat sniffs the pup. The pup sits on his back legs and pants and licks his fat lips. Then he lands on his back and flings his legs up. The cat thinks this is funny. Then the pup sits up and hugs his chum.

❧ LESSON **THIRTY-ONE** ❧

Introduce the single letter consonant sound **j** (as in **jog**) and the capital letter **J** and *blend*.

[Note: the letter **j** is usually found at the beginning of a word; when the sound **j** is found at the end of a word it is denoted by **dge** (as in **badge**) or **ge** (as in **age**). Sometimes the sound **j** is found within words when it is denoted by the letters **dj** (as in **adjust**).]

1. **Read, write and practise:**

jam	**jab**
jig	**jilt**
jog	**jolly**
jet	**jelly**
jug	**jumpy**
Jim	**Jan**

2. **Add j to the following and practise:**

....**am**	....**ab**	....**et**
....**ug**	....**ob**	....**ig**
....**elly**	....**olly**	....**umpy**

3. **Read the following sentences:**

> **Milk is in a jug.**
> **Jets fly in the sky.**
> **Jilly had jelly at lunch.**
> **The jolly puppy jumps up.**
> **Fetch fresh jam buns from the tin.**

4. **Read:**

> **A jolly fish is swimming in a pond. This is not a jelly fish. This fish can flip his fins up and run rings on the pond. Fish cannot sink and vanish. Fish pops his head up and blinks at a red robin sitting on the bank munching a nut. This is his lunch. Then the jolly robin puffs up his fat tummy and sings. Fish gulps and swims off. Such a jolly fish is swimming in a pond and such a jolly robin is sitting on a twig.**

❧ LESSON **THIRTY-TWO** ❧

Revise the plural form of the consonant sound **k** (as in **socks**) and introduce this same sound denoted by the single letter **x** (as in the **fox**). Practise *blending*.

1. **Read, write and practise:**

> sack → sacks
> sock → socks
> stick → sticks

x	x	x
tax	wax	fax
fix	six	mix
ox	box	fox
vex	ax	Rex
fixing	mixing	boxing

2. **Add x to the following and practise:**

bo___	fo___	mi___
si___	ta___	wa___
fi___	ve___	e___it

3. **Add ing to the following and practise:**

tax___	fix___	wax___
vex___	box___	mix___

4. **Read:**

A fluffy red fox sits in a den with six fluffy pups. It is sunny and fresh. Fox pops up and sniffs. Fox yaps and jumps with the six red cubs on the fresh soft sand. It is hot. The cubs yelp and crack twigs and jump up. Suddenly fox stops and sniffs a smell in the strong fresh wind. It tells fox that a man is in the forest with his dog. The canny fox has hidden the six fox cubs in the den. The cubs cannot run and yap but sit still in the den with mum. Fox has twigs and sticks on the exit and a man cannot get in.

The man and his black dog run up. The dog sniffs but a duck flaps his wings and jumps up from a pond. The dog runs on. The man sits a bit on a rock. Then the man stands up and slings his gun on his back. Then canny fox tells the six jolly cubs that a fox and a big hunting dog cannot frolic as friends.

Introduce the long vowel sound **e** (as in **bee** and **tea**) and *blend*.

[Note: the same vowel sound in **field**, **shield**, **thief** and **grief**.]

1. **Read, write and practise:**

ee	ee	ee
bee	see	seen
tree	feet	deep
keep	seek	feed
sweep	sweet	sleep
weep	creep	green
sheep	sheet	street
peep	three	free

2. **Add ee to the following and practise:**

s_____	tr_____	gr_____n
b_____	fr_____	sl_____p
m_____t	w_____k	k_____p

3. **Read the following sentences:**

A bee can sting.
Candy is sweet.
Three sheep sleep at his feet.

**Green trees stand in the grand street.
Miss Streep can see Dee sweeping the
street.**

4. Read:

A cat creeps up a big green tree and sits happily.
The cat sees a red robin. Then the cat jumps
up on his feet and creeps up. The cat is three
steps from the robin and is licking his lips.

5. Read, write and practise:

ea	ea	ea
neat	seat	heat
team	beam	dream
cream	steal	veal
speak	cheap	teach
peach	meal	real
eat	each	treat

6. Add **ea** to the following and practise:

dr___m   l___f   gl___m

n___t   s___t   r___l

sp___k   ch___p   cr___m

7. Read the following sentences:

Speak up.

Teach him a lot.

This peach is not cheap.

This meal with veal is a real treat.

In the hot sun the sea is a still flat pond.

At the wedding Pat had a peach and cream hat on.

8. Read:

A tramp is sitting on a bench and eating a cheap meal. It is not a pink peach and it is not red meat. It is a jam bun. A sea gull lands on the next seat and gets a real treat from the tramp.

9. Now practise **ee** and **ea**:

ee	ea
ee	**ea**
see	**sea**
meet	**meat**
week	**weak**
peel	**peal**
seem	**seam**
teem	**team**
flee	**flea**
beech	**beach**
reel	**real**

10. Now try these:

Yasmin sleeps and dreams.
In the hot sun he feels the heat.
Teach him sums this week.
This green dress has seams.

Dee sees a free man in the street.
The sand on the beach is soft and deep.

Feel the soft wind on the cheek.
Dream sweet dreams and feel free.

❧ LESSON **THIRTY-FOUR** ❧

Revise the long vowel sound **e** (as in **bee** and **tea**). Introduce the same long vowel sound **e** (as in **me**) and *blend*.

1. **Read, write, and practise:**

me	
he	He
she	She
we	We
be	Be

2. **Read the following sentences:**

Be happy.
Be jolly.
Tell me.
Send me that hat.
He can sing.
He is glad.
We can fly.
We will not cry.
She is a duchess.
She is rich.

3. Add **he** or **she** to the following sentences and practise:

Tom is funny. .... is funny.
Tess is funny. .... is funny.
Fred is a dad. .... is a dad.
Fran is a mum. .... is a mum.
Dee has a dolly. .... has a dolly.
.... is a lad. .... is a lass.

4. Add **me** to the following sentences and practise:

Tell ....
Bring ....
Free ....
Set .... up.
Back .... up.
Hand .... a cup.

5. Add **we** to the following sentences and practise:

.... can run.
.... can jump.
.... can skip.
.... can swim.
Shall .... sing?
Shall .... eat?
Shall .... peep?

6. **Now try these sentences:**

> **She is seeing him next week.**
> **She is not strong. She is weak.**
>
> **He is unhappy and seems unwell.**
> **The pink dress has seams.**
>
> **She must flee from the big dog.**
> **A flea bit him.**
>
> **She felt the sting of a bee on the cheek.**
> **Let me be with him at the tea shop.**
>
> **A beech tree stands at the end of the street.**
> **On the beach we can feel the hot sand.**
>
> **If it is hot we shall meet next week at the seaside.**
> **She can see fresh meat in the shop.**
>
> **We cannot sip really hot tea – can we?**

7. Read:

Figgy the frog has a dream. In his dream he jumps the longest and best jump and he is the biggest and best frog in the pond. Figgy sits on a flat leaf and tells Fred Fish his dream. Fred chats with frog and tells him his plan. Figgy must jump big jumps. Then he will be top frog in the pond and his dream will be real. Figgy sits still. Then he huffs and puffs his fat belly up. He jumps as much as he can. Fred Fish flaps ten flaps with his fins and Figgy jumps ten jumps. This is such fun. Fred Fish claps his fins on his back. Figgy will be top frog for real and not just in his dream.

❧ LESSON **THIRTY-FIVE** ❧

Introduce the long vowel sound **a** (as in **say** and **sail**) and *blend*.

[Note: the same vowel sound in **they**, **prey**, **grey** and **neigh**.]

1. **Read, write and practise:**

ay	ay	ay
say	day	pay
play	way	ray
hay	bay	may
stay	tray	pray
stray	spray	clay
slay	Kay	May

2. **Add ay to the following and practise:**

s............	tr............	d............
p............	st............	sl............
m............	w............	b............

3. **Read the following sentences:**

Stay with me.
I can pay him cash.
May we stay and play?
Kay plays in the team.
Sunday is a fun day.

4. **Read, write and practise:**

ai	ai	ai
sail	tail	mail
pail	rail	fail
rain	pain	plain
paid	maid	trail
train	grain	chain

5. **Add ai to the following and practise:**

s......l	tr......n	r......n
p......n	st......n	sl......n
m......l	t......l	ch......n

6. **Read the following sentences:**

A dog wags his tail.
He is in pain.
Rain is fresh and clean.
Sail upstream.
He paid the bill promptly.

In his sleep he dreams and in his dream he sails the seven seas.

7. **Read:**

> A duck with a green and black tail sees the raindrops. It is not a sunny day in May. It is a wet and rainy Sunday. Raindrops splash on the pond. Duck thinks it is silly sitting on the bank and waiting. She thinks a rainy day is fun. She flaps off in the deep end. Rain is fresh and clean. The pond is a big tea cup with raindrops on top.
>
> A big black stray dog with a waggy tail jumps in the pond and gets wet. He swims. Duck cannot play with such a big splash and such a big dog. She waits until the wet dog ends his swim. Then she drinks the fresh raindrops and swims.

8. **Now read this sentence:**

> **The rain in Spain stays mainly in the plain.**

❦ LESSON **THIRTY-SIX** ❦

Revise the long vowel sound **i** (as in **fly**) ☞ see **Lesson 24**.
Introduce the same long vowel sound **i** (as in **tie**) and **igh** (as in **sigh**) and *blend*.

1. **Revise:**

my	by
sky	cry
dry	try
fly	shy

2. **Read, write and practise:**

ie	ie
pie	pies
tie	ties
die	dies
dry	dries
try	tries
cry	cries
fly	flies
fry	fries

3. **Add ie to the following and practise:**

    p......s   t......s   d......s
    tr......s   cr......s   fl......s

4.   Read the following sentences:

> I eat meat pies and French fries.
> He tries fried eggs and chips.
> Dried twigs lie by the tree.
> My mum cries if she is sad.
> We must not tell lies.
> Try and see it my way.
> Sit by me and try this sum.

5.   Read, write, and practise:

sigh	high	sight
light	might	right
fight	flight	fright
night	plight	slight

6.   Add **igh** to the following and practise:

s_____   h_____   n_____t

l_____t   s_____t   fl_____t

7. **Read the following sentences:**

> **The sun is high and bright and brings light.**
>
> **Gulls can be seen high up in the trees.**
>
> **He must not fight with his mum. It is not right.**
>
> **The right way cannot be seen in the night.**
>
> **A happy man sleeps well at night.**

Revise the long vowel sound **i** (as in **tie** and **sigh**). Introduce the same long vowel sound **i** (as in **mild**) and the personal pronoun **I**. Practise *blending*.

[Note: the two different vowel sounds of the word "**wind**" which denote different meanings.]

1. **Read, write and practise:**

mild	wild	child
mind	kind	find
rind	blind	bind
grind	wind	unwind

2. **Add i to the following and practise:**

m___nd	k___nd	f___nd
m___ld	w___ld	ch___ld
b___nd	bl___nd	unk___nd

3. **Read the following sentences:**

Mind the steps.
He is kind.
She is a shy and timid child.
A blind man cannot see.
Stray dogs can be wild.
It is a mild day in May.
She has a free mind.

4. **Practise the personal pronoun I:**

I am	**I can**	**I shall**
I will	**I may**	**I sing**
I play	**I see**	**I speak**
I try	**I sigh**	**I mind**

I am speaking.

I am not telling lies.

I shall be feeling glad on Sunday.

I am a free man. I can think. I can speak and I can read.

He is a free man. He can think. He can speak and read.

5. **Practise the following longer words:**

blindness	**kindness**	**wildness**
childless	**unkindness**	**mindlessness**

❧ LESSON **THIRTY-EIGHT** ❧

Introduce the long vowel sound **o** as in (**goat** and **glow**) and a small number of useful words which denote the same long vowel sound by different letter combinations. Practise *blending*.

[Note the phonic irregularity: "How now brown cow!" ☞ see **Lesson 56**.]

1. **Read, write and practise:**

oa	oa	oa
soap	goat	moat
soak	goal	load
boat	gloat	throat
road	toast	boast

2. **Add oa to the following and practise:**

s......p	g......l	g......t
s......k	b......t	l......d

3. **Read the following sentences:**

> My goal is in sight.
> A goat is eating a green leaf.
> The mild soap is in this box.
>
> The team wins the match with a goal.

4. **Read, write and practise:**

low	mow	tow
row	slow	flow
glow	blow	snow
grow	rowing	window

5. **Add ow to the following and practise:**

l........	gl........	bl........
sn........	sl........	gr........

6. **Read the following sentences:**

The sun is low in the sky.

The sun glows dimly in the low light.
I will grow up and be in the top team.
On the pond the snow flows slowly as it melts.

7. **Now try these words which sound the same but are spelt differently:**

go	no	so
most	post	host
toe	toes	goes
though		

8. Read the following sentences:

> **He goes up the steps quickly.**
> **He steps on his toes as he goes.**
>
> **I am old and my hands feel the cold.**
> **Hold the box with this gold ring in it.**

9. Read:

> **I go up the dimly lit road. It is so cold. The snow lands on the street and the trees. The snow is not wet. It is fresh cold snow and it gleams and glows. The lights in the street lamps glow so low that the traffic flows by me slowly. An old man greets me as I go up the road. I dream of hot toast as I blow on my cold hands and see the frost showing up on the old windows.**

✤ LESSON **THIRTY-NINE** ✤

Revise the long vowel sound **a** (as in **say** and **sail**) ☛ see **Lesson 35**. Introduce the same long vowel sound **a** (as in **fate**) and *blend*.

[Rule: the silent **e** changes the short vowel sound **a** (as in **fat**) to the long vowel sound **a** (as in **fate**). Note the exception ☛ **have**. In addition, note that silent **e** added to the consonant **r** changes the short vowel **a** in a slightly different way (as in **rare**).]

1. **Read, write and practise:**

ate	ale	late
date	gate	fate
hate	mate	pate
rate	plate	pale
tale	dale	gale
dame	game	tame
lame	shame	make
lake	take	shake
lane	fade	trade
grade	pave	cave
cake	Jane	Dave

2.   **Read the following sentences:**

Dave hates green jelly and cakes.
The rusty gate by the lake is shut.

Let the plate with the cake on it stay on the tray.
Make me happy by playing that game with him.
Jane is late but she can still make the grade.

The puppy has a fluffy tail.
Tell me a tale with a happy ending.

A man is a male.
Let me take the mail and post it.

The wet rag is still in the pail.
She has been sick and is pale.

Spend cash in the sale.
Ships sail the high seas.

3. **Now try these:**

fat	fate
hat	hate
mat	mate
pat	pate
rat	rate
mad	made
fad	fade
glad	glade
pal	pale
pan	pane
can	cane
man	mane
Sam	same
Jan	Jane

4. Sometimes words which sound the same are spelt differently. Here are some examples:

sail	sale
tail	tale
pail	pale
mail	male
hail	hale
bail	bale
Gail	gale
pain	pane
main	mane

5. Here are some words which sound a little different because they contain the consonant r. Practise them separately:

dare	rare	care
bare	glare	stare
air	pair	hair
fair	lair	stair
pear	bear	wear

❧ LESSON **FORTY** ❧

Revise the long vowel sound **i** (as in **pie** and **sigh**) ☞ see **Lesson 36**. Introduce the same long vowel sound **i** (as in **fine**) and *blend*.

[Rule: the silent **e** changes the short vowel sound **i** (as in **fin**) to the long vowel sound **i** (as in **fine**). Note the exceptions ☞ **give** and the verb **"to live"**.]

1. **Read, write and practise:**

mine	pine	fine
wine	shine	line
twine	spine	bite
kite	spite	side
hide	slide	ride
tide	time	slime
like	pipe	ripe
swipe	stripe	spite
hike	pike	spike

2. **Read the following sentences:**

She drank sweet red wine.
Add a fine thin line at the end.
I like fine wine but I dislike figs.
He flies his kite high in the sky.
A fish has fine fins.
When I win at chess I feel fine.

The shin is at the front of the leg.

We spent a lot of time playing hide and seek.

Pine trees stand by the side of the road.

The moon shines its bright light on the pond.

3.   Read:

It is a fine day in May. Ben is sitting on a bench and sees a plane flying by. It shines high in the sunlit sky. Ben likes the flying plane. The next day Ben takes his kite. It is made with thin strips of ply and string. He pretends that the kite is a plane. He runs up the hill with his dog Fluff by his side. Fluff huffs and puffs as he tries jogging on his short fat legs. Dry twigs snap as he trots by.

Ben lets his kite fly off. It trails its tail like a real flying plane. It is a fine sight. Then the string snaps. Ben cries as his fine kite flies off. But Fluff runs on. He will try and find the kite. Ben sits on the bench and waits. He is upset. Will Fluff get my kite thinks Ben sadly? The dry twigs snap as Fluff brings the kite up and drops it by the bench. Ben jumps up and pats his dog. Fluff yaps happily and Ben is as happy and bright as Fluff. Ben can mend the kite and

tie the string back. Then he will try and fly it the next day.

4. **Now try these:**

pin	pine
fin	fine
shin	shine
win	wine
bit	bite
slid	slide
pip	pipe
twin	twine
spin	spine
spit	spite
strip	stripe
hid	hide

❦ LESSON **FORTY-ONE** ❦

Revise the long vowel sound **o** (as in **goat** and **glow**) ☞ see **Lesson 38**. Introduce the long vowel sound **o** (as in **note**) and *blend*.

[Rule: the silent **e** changes the short vowel **o** (as in **not**) to the long vowel sound **o** (as in **note**). Note the phonic exceptions ☞ **love** and **gone** and the spelling exceptions ☞ **rogue** and **vogue**.]

1. **Read, write and practise:**

note	**dote**	**vote**
rote	**rode**	**rope**
dole	**hole**	**pole**
mole	**stole**	**robe**
lone	**home**	**dome**

2. **Read the following sentences:**

She can take the high note.
He rode back on his bike.
We do not smoke at home.
I hope I can vote on Sunday.

Take this note and send it on by post.
The mole made a big hole and hid.
At the stroke of midnight the bells ring.

3. **Read:**

> Spotkin is a fine dog. He is black. At home he has a bed with a spotty red rug on it. It is soft and fluffy. He hopes he gets a bone. He likes to sniff it. Then he takes it and hides it in a hole. Spotkin runs and jumps but he cannot hop like a frog. He trots up to me and I rub his tummy. He hates it if I am late home. He hates it when it rains and his feet get wet in the cold. I like my pet a lot. At home Spotkin sits at my feet and I am not lonely.

4. **Now try these:**

not	note
rob	robe
hop	hope
cod	code
pop	Pope
Tom	tome

5. Here are some common words with a silent **e** which are exceptions:

> **love**
>
> **gone**
>
> **done**
>
> **live**
>
> **give**
>
> **have**

6. Now try these:

> **We have gone to visit his sick chum.**
>
> **We hope to give him a gift.**
>
> **I love fluffy pink rabbits.**
>
> **Live and let live.**
>
> **The grand duke loves red wine.**
>
> **We love plum jam and plum cake.**
>
> **The rocket has gone to the moon.**
>
> **We must give him a big clap if he wins the match.**

🦋 LESSON **FORTY-TWO** 🦋

Introduce the long vowel sound **u** (as in **cute**) and *blend*.

[Rule: the silent **e** changes the short vowel sound **u** (as in **cut**) to the long vowel sound **u** (as in **cute**).

1. **Read, write and practise:**

cute	tune	mute
mule	dune	duke
fumes	dispute	dupe

2. **Read the following sentences:**

   The puppy is cute.
   A mute cannot speak.
   We sing in tune.
   I hate disputes.
   A duke sits in his grand home.

   He rode his mule on the sand dunes by the sea.

3. **Read:**

   A cute green frog sits on a leaf floating on a deep green pond and croaks. Figgy the frog likes this pond. He thinks it is as big as a lake. It is not. It is wide and deep and Figgy feels just like a duke in his grand home.

Figgy sits on a lily pad and hums. He is not silent and mute. He hums happily but he cannot sing in tune. He is a fine frog with long green legs but his tune has lots of funny notes in it. In fact he croaks. It is not a sweet tune. It is just a funny froggy song with deep notes in it.

❦ LESSON **FORTY-THREE** ❦

Revise the consonant sound **w** (as in **wet**) ☞ see **Lesson 20**. Introduce the same consonant sound **w** (as in **when**) and *blend*.

[Note the phonic exception: **wh** + **at** ☞ **what** (as in **was** and **because**).]

1. **Read, write and practise:**

when	where	whim
whip	whiff	whist
whisk	while	why

2. **Add wh to the following and practise:**

........en	........im	........iff
........y	........isk	........ist

3. **Read the following sentences:**

> **I went when I had time.**
> **Where is the shop?**
> **Where can we sit?**
> **Whist is a game we can play.**
> **Whisk the fresh eggs.**
> **Why is this on?**
> **Why has she left?**
>
> **Whip the cream when he brings the coffee in.**

4. **Practise this word and then read the sentences:**

> **what**
>
> **What is this?**
> **What can he say?**
> **What is she singing?**
> **What is he eating?**
> **What is on his plate?**
> **What kind of play is he in?**

❧ LESSON **FORTY-FOUR** ❧

Introduce the long vowel soon **oo** (as in **moon**) and a small number of useful words which denote the same long vowel sound by different letter combinations ☛ **do**, **to**, **two**, **you**, **who**, **whom**, **whose** and **lose**. Practise *blending*.

1. Read, write and practise:

cool	**pool**	**soon**
moon	**mood**	**boot**
noon	**hoot**	**root**
spool	**spoon**	**shoot**
too	**tool**	**tooth**

2. Add oo to the following and practise:

n........n	**m........n**	**sp........n**
m........d	**p........l**	**s........n**

3. Read the following sentences:

Silk is soft and smooth.
At noon it is hot.
I sit still and keep cool.
I am not in a bad mood.
The maid sweeps the room.
Jump in the cool pool.

4. Read:

> Gary dreams a dream. It is high noon and he is sitting on the moon. Soon he sees hills and a thin wispy mist. Black rocks stand at his feet and the moon hills seem cool. A thin pink mist tints a pool and from the pool runs a thin stream. In this moody dream moon frogs with big black spots swing on pink trees growing from the cool sand.
>
> Gary sees a moon buggy. He jumps in and drives on. He keeps up with the stream. At the rim of a red hill he sees a tent. It has a blue tint and stands on the cool sand. It is held with green rope and wide pink silk strands. It is like a dome.
>
> Gary thinks the king of the moon must be in the tent. He stands up on his moon buggy seat and sings a moon song as a greeting. Soon he will wake up and see that he has been dreaming a foolish but happy dream.

5. **Practise these words and then read the sentences:**

do   **to**   **too**
you   **whom**   **whose**
lose

Do you eat fish and chips?
It is silly to do it.
Do two sums too.
Who is standing at the back?
Whom will you pick?
Whose pen is this?

You must not lose the two pens I lent you.

What will you do when you lose too?

❧ LESSON **FORTY-FIVE** ❧

Revise the long vowel sound **oo** (as in **moon**) ☞ see **Lesson 44**. Introduce the same long vowel sound **ew** (as in **grew**) and **ue** (as in **blue**). Practise *blending*.

1. **Read, write and practise:**

    grew   crew   brew
    chew   flew   threw

2. **Add ew to the following and practise:**

    ch........   **gr**........   **fl**........

3. **Read the following sentences:**

    The birds flew high up in the sky.
    He chews his food a long time.

    He grew up and we will grow up too.
    She threw the rug on the bed.

    When she lost the game she threw the racket up and ran off.

    The weeds grew and grew and grew in the heat.

4. **Read, write, and practise:**

> **blue** **glue** **true**
> **cue** **clue** **Sue**

5. **Add ue to the following and practise:**

> **bl**............ **gl**............ **tr**............

6. **Read the following sentences:**

> **A blue sky shines on a blue sea.**
> **Tell me this is true.**
> **You can glue it back with glue.**
> **Sue is a true chum.**

7. **Read:**

> **Ben has his best blue pants and his best blue hat on. He likes blue. He cleans his teeth with a blue tooth brush and he has blue soap. He plays with pink and blue balloons.**

> **He sees a man painting with a spray gun. Ben thinks this is fun. He takes the spray gun and fills it with blue paint. He can then spray blue paint on the trees and he can spray his boots blue. He can make blue chewing gum and drink blue milk.**

> **Luckily his mum spots him just as he takes the new blue gun from the shed.**

❧ LESSON **FORTY-SIX** ❧

Introduce the short vowel sound **oo** (as in **book**) and a small number of useful words which denote the same short vowel sound by different letter combinations ☞ **put**, **push**, **pull**, **full**, **bull**, **would**, **could** and **should**. Practise *blending*.

[Note: the short vowel sound **oo** often precedes the letter **k**.]

1. **Read, write and practise:**

book	**cook**	**look**
took	**brook**	**crook**
soot	**foot**	**good**

2. **Add oo to the following and practise:**

t___k	**l___k**	**b___k**
c___k	**cr___k**	**g___d**
h___k	**r___k**	**n___k**

3. **Read the following sentences:**

> **Look at the book.**
> **The crook took a good look.**
> **A brook is like a stream.**
> **I can kick with my foot.**
> **Look at the sunset.**
> **The green pond looks pink.**
> **She took the gift.**
> **Gran cooks good food.**
> **We will read good books soon.**
> **Cool silk is smooth.**

4. **Practise these words and then read the sentences:**

	put	
	push	
pull	**full**	**bull**
would	**could**	**should**

> **Put it in the book.**
> **The cup is full.**
> **Pull the blind up and let the sun in.**
> **I would help you if I could.**
> **I should do it soon.**
> **Should he take the book back?**
> **Push it up the hill.**

❧ LESSON **FORTY-SEVEN** ❧

Introduce the long neutral stressed **er** sound (as in **herd**, **bird** and **turn**) and *blend*.

1. **Read, write and practise:**

her	herd	perm
pert	perch	Gertrude

fir	bird	girl
dirt	shirt	first
birch	third	stir

fur	turn	curl
burn	hurt	slur
spurt	church	purr

2. **Read the following sentences:**

Wet twigs cannot burn.
Fir trees stay green.
His team came first.
Fire burns.
Turn the tap on.
Cats purr.

The bird sits on his perch on a birch tree.

The girl curls up on her soft rug and sleeps.

3. **Read:**

Soft green ferns sway by the pool and the old church. High trees stand by the old church too. The first tree I see is a fir tree. Next I turn my head and see a birch tree in bloom. Birch trees bloom in spring. I see birds perching on a branch.

By the church I see a girl in a fur hat and a thick red skirt.

❧ LESSON **FORTY-EIGHT** ❧

Introduce the short neutral unstressed **er** sound (as in **sister**, **doctor** and **China**) and *blend*.

[Note: this short neutral unstressed sound is found in the indefinite and definite articles (**"a"** and **"the"**) ☞ see **Lesson 26**.]

1. Read, write and practise:

sister	**letter**	**better**
fatter	**winter**	**matter**
backer	**lobster**	**thinner**
bigger	**longer**	**shorter**
stronger	**teacher**	**summer**

2. Add **er** to the following and practise:

teach.........	**clean**.........	**crack**.........
dream.........	**think**.........	**paint**.........
short.........	**long**.........	**strong**.........
weak.........	**clever**.........	**kind**.........

3. Read the following sentences:

> **It is colder in winter than in summer.**
> **She looks thinner in the longer dress.**
> **The teacher is stricter than her sister.**
> **The rubber band gets longer and longer.**
> **It is cooler by the pool and hotter in the room.**

4. Read, write and practise:

actor	**editor**	**doctor**
visitor	**professor**	**emperor**
inspector	**instructor**	**director**

5. Add **or** to the following and practise:

act.........	**inspect**.........	**doct**.........
visit.........	**direct**.........	**edit**.........

6. Read the following sentences:

> **Visitors must check in at the lobby.**
> **Professors can teach too.**
> **A doctor visits the sick.**
> **The actor plays the emperor.**
> **The driving instructor teaches a lot.**
> **The inspector came.**

7. **Read, write and practise:**

China	**India**	**Panama**
Canada	**Kenya**	**Japan**

8. **Now try these:**

along	**amend**	**away**
across	**afresh**	**alone**
amiss	**afraid**	**abide**

9. **Read:**

Jimmy and I spend a lot of time at my home on the river bank. Jimmy is a retired professor. He is very old. He is a kind and clever man. Long ago when he was twenty he was an opera singer and actor. He was richer and slimmer and stronger. Then he spent a long time studying the lives of fur trappers and fisherman in Lapland and living in an igloo.

When it is winter he sits like an old emperor on a settee by the open log fire with a fur rug across his legs.

I hope the holiday arrives sooner rather than later and I can persuade Jimmy to stay the winter at my home on the river bank.

1. **Read, write and practise:**

toil	soil	boil
foil	coil	coin
join	joint	point

2. **Add oi to the following and practise:**

   c........n   b........l   p........nt

   c........l   embr........l   t........l

3. **Read the following sentences:**

   I join in the song.
   A snake can coil itself up.
   Trees can grow well in moist soil.

   If we boil eggs too long we spoil them.

4. **Read, write and practise:**

boy	toy	joy
enjoy	ploy	employ
coy	Roy	Troy

5. Add **oy** to the following and practise:

   b............   j............   t............

6. Read the following sentences:

   Boys and girls enjoy toy shops.
   The director employs actors.
   Helen of Troy enjoys fame.
   Roy has a boy and is full of joy.

7. Read:

   Joanna cooks a joint. She will not burn the meat. She boils the carrots and greens in a big pan. She can make a hotpot too.

   Joanna tells Roy to stop playing with his toys and join gran and the rest of the family at dinner. We shall enjoy the dinner for it is a joy to eat.

❧ LESSON **FIFTY** ❧

Introduce the long vowel sound **a** (as in **car** and **bath**) and *blend*.

[Note the phonic exception ☛ **are** (the present tense of the verb to be).]

1. **Read, write and practise:**

car	bar	far
jar	arm	harm
farm	bark	lark
mark	park	barn
harp	arch	dart
part	start	sharp
last	past	mast
bath	path	pass
grass	brass	art
varnish	sparkling	star

2. **Read the following sentences:**

The big dog will bark if you scream.
I shall mark the book.
Teach me to play the harp.
The park is in the dark.
The sun is a star.
Hollywood is far from me.

The art book is a gift.
We can see fish darting about.
Freddy can polish and varnish the car.
The sparkling lake in the park is not muddy.

3. Read:

It is dark. Sparkling stars glow like silver dots in the deep black sky. It is a bit spooky. A car looms up. Its lamps glow and then grow dim as the driver turns the lights off.

The driver is home. He stops and looks up at the glowing stars. The moon looks like a big white boat as it floats by.

He darts up the steps by the front gate and sees his cat sitting on the garden path waiting for him. The cat is hurt and cannot jump up. The man picks his cat up and tucks him in his coat. He strides inside.

Introduce the digraph **au** which is denoted by many letter combinations ☛ (as in **for**, **talk** and **law**). Introduce some further common letter combinations for the digraph **au** ☛ **four**, **door**, **broad**, **caught** and **bought**. Practise *blending*.

1. **Read, write and practise:**

for	fork	cork
pork	lord	cord
ford	fort	form
sort	sport	short
corn	story	glory
forty	sporty	north
born	inform	forlorn

2. **Read the following sentences:**

Read me a short story.

Forty winks is not a long sleep.

Pork is meat from a pig.

Be a good sport.

Forlorn means unhappy.

Inform me when you can.

The compass points north.

The fort on top of the hill is strong.

3. **Read, write and practise:**

talk	walk	stalk
chalk	halt	salt
tall	call	ball
fall	wall	small
stall	hall	all

4. **Read the following sentences:**

We can talk all day long.

Tell me when he calls.

Jim had a bad fall.

The tramp walks with a limp.

Stop talking.

Tom is a tall boy and he will be a taller man.

Stand by the wall and catch the ball.

5. **Read, write and practise:**

law	paw	saw
jaw	raw	fawn
pawn	lawn	straw
yawn	shawl	crawl

6. **Read the following sentences:**

> **Cook the raw eggs.**
> **I yawn when I am sleepy.**
> **I saw them walking up the steps.**
> **Bambi was a fawn.**
> **Before you walk you crawl.**

7. **Now try these common words which are spelt differently:**

four	**door**	**floor**
broad	**war**	**water**
fault	**cause**	

caught	**daughter**	**naughty**

ought	**bought**	**brought**
fought	**nought**	

❧ LESSON **FIFTY-TWO** ❧

Introduce and practise adding **-ed** at the end of verbs.

[Rule: **-ed** is always sounded as a separate syllable if it follows the letters **t** or **d** (as in **noted** and **added**); it is not sounded as a separate syllable when it is added to any other letter (as in **filled** and **kissed**).]

1. **Read, write and practise:**

   act → acted   love → loved
   date → dated   live → lived
   blend → blended   kiss → kissed
   note → noted   miss → missed
   vote → voted   tick → ticked
   fit → fitted   blink → blinked
   lift → lifted   pin → pinned
   paint → painted   back → backed
   mend → mended   rock → rocked
   hate → hated   cook → cooked

2. **Read the following sentences:**

   He acted in a West End play.
   His eyes blinked from the bright light.

   The boys voted for the teacher.
   Mum cooked the yummy dinner.

Dad painted the bedroom yellow.
The dog lived in his kennel.

Paul mended the broken box.
The dog loved his master.

3. **Read:**

 Astra took part in a play. She acted in a comedy. She was excited. Her costume was made of velvet.

She noted that it was time to get dressed for the part. She was thrilled as she fitted her dress on.

On the platform she lived her part to the full and loved it. After the play she slept very well all night long.

1. Read, write and practise:

able	table	cable
fable	sable	stable

tangle	mangle	spangle
rabble	dabble	strangle

little	brittle	fiddle
thimble	nimble	swindle

bottle	gobble	wobble
kettle	settle	nettle

bubble	puddle	muddle
cuddle	rubble	huddle

2. Read:

Molly sits at the table. She is able but today Molly is in a muddle. She broke a milk bottle. She got her skipping rope in a tangle. She lost her little thimble. When she sat at the table she giggled. Her tummy made a rumble. Molly is still in a silly muddle.

❧ LESSON **FIFTY-FOUR** ❧

Introduce the soft consonant sound **c** (as in **ace**) and *blend*.

[Note the phonic irregularity ☛ **once**.]

1. **Read, write and practise:**

ace	face	lace
race	space	grace
ice	mice	nice
spice	twice	thrice
suffice	advice	dice
dance	chance	glance
prance	enhance	France
mince	since	prince
pence	fence	Spencer
	once	

2. **Read the following sentences:**

The pond has thick ice on it.
Ice-cream is nice.
I read the book twice.
Thrice will suffice.

The cat chases the mice.

The girl has a kind face.

The wedding dress is made of lace.

Grace likes to race.

I can dance the tango.

Let us visit France which is nice in spring time.

Since he has lost his licence he cannot drive.

In a short space of time the Spice Girls will sing.

Once upon a time a princess went to Iceland.

Just by chance I had the ace of spades in my hand.

Shall we dance?

❦ LESSON **FIFTY-FIVE** ❦

Introduce the soft consonant sound **g** (as in **gem**, **age** and **ledge**).
☛ see Note in **Lesson 31**. Practise *blending*.

1. **Read, write and practise:**

gem	gel	gender
gentle	gentleman	gently
geology	generosity	geometry

age	page	cage
wage	rage	sage
stage	range	strange
change	exchange	danger

badge	hedge	ledge
fridge	bridge	lodge
dodge	judge	grudge

2. **Read the following sentences:**

Age is not important.
The bird sings in its cage.
The first page is interesting.
The stage is empty.
A fridge is a cold place.
Cross the bridge when it is dark.

Trim the hedge.
He must change his strange ways.
Read the first page once.
The ice age came a long time ago.

3. Read:

Once upon a time a lovely princess lived in a wonderfully strange palace in Iceland. The princess kept a bird. She fed it on rice and grains and seeds. It lived in a nice cage in her garden but when it became too cold in the long dark winter nights she let the bird fly away to a nicer place.

After many long winter nights the bird flew back to the princess in her strange palace. It landed on the ledge and sang. Once again the kind princess gave it rice and grains and seeds and once again the princess was happy.

❧ LESSON **FIFTY-SIX** ❧

Introduce the diphthong **ou** (as in **round** and **owl**) and *blend*.

1. **Read, write and practise:**

loud	**cloud**	**spout**
trout	**round**	**found**
sound	**pound**	**shout**
pouch	**south**	**mouth**
house	**mouse**	**out**

2. **Add ou to the following and practise:**

sc____t   m____th   p____nd
h____nd   ____tlook   ____tlaw

3. **Read the following sentences:**

Shouting makes a loud sound.
A mouse is in the house.
The clouds went south.
He found a round stone.

4. **Read, write and practise:**

owl	growl	howl
town	frown	gown
brown	now	cow
how	flower	power
shower	tower	drowsy

5. **Add ow to the following and practise:**

t......n   fr......n   gr......l

h......   c......   n......

6. **Read the following sentences:**

A brown owl sits in the barn.
Cows give milk.
Now the king has no power.
Trouts frolic when it showers.
He frowned at the loud sound.

He paces up and down his town house.
Crowds run round the shops in town.
A crowd of boy scouts went round the houses.

7. **Read:**

It is dark by the round pond out of town. It is late. No sound rises from the silent house. I look up and see shooting stars that sparkle and shine in the dark. I like it outside the house in the garden at this time. It is cool. The thick grand firs and pines make a spooky outline at the south gate. There are no crowds about at this time and no one shouts.

Then the moon peeps out and shines. It gleams and without a sound a cat creeps up. It lifts its face to the pale moon and winks at the stars. An owl hoots. The cat howls. I return to the house without a sound.

❧ LESSON **FIFTY-SEVEN** ❧

Introduce the **shun** sound (as in **nation** and **pension**) and *blend*.

[Note: in itself, the **shun** sound cannot be considered one of the 44 sounds since it is a *blend* of these three sounds ☞ **sh** + **u** + **n**. However, it is surely most convenient to practise this particular *blending* as one sound denoted by an easily identifiable combination of letters.]

1. **Read, write and practise:**

nation	station	action
mention	diction	fiction
faction	friction	invention
creation	relaxation	ration
operation	function	junction
tension	pension	mansion
expansion	session	mission
	fashion	

2. **Add tion to the following and practise:**

men............   fic............

dic............   inven............

ac............   erup............

3. add **sion** to the following and practise:

man............   ten............

pen............   expan............

exten............   comprehen............

4. Read the following sentences:

The train is standing at the station.

This mansion is huge.

Fiction is an invention.

Tension brings pain.

Relaxation brings satisfaction.

His dad is sixty-five and is given a pension.

5. Read:

At the top of a hill stands a mansion. It is the home of a rich and silent man. His name is Count Magoo. He is a great inventor. His invention is a silent plane that can fly in the silence of the sky. He is a man of vision. His mansion is his creation. It is dark and gloomy. Not a sound escapes.

6. Now try these common words which sound a little different:

vision   **revision**   **division**

precision   **television**   **collision**

❦ LESSON **FIFTY-EIGHT** ❦

Introduce the **zh** sound (as in **pleasure**) and the **ch** sound (as in **picture**) and *blend*.

1. **Read, write and practise:**

> pleasure   measure   treasure
> measurement   leisure

2. **Read the following sentences:**

> **Treasure lay on the sea bed.**
> **I treasure this gift.**
> **My leisure time is well spent.**
>
> **Measure her waist with a tape measure.**
> **I found much pleasure in reading this book.**

3. **Read, write and practise:**

> picture   mixture   puncture
> fracture   gesture   fixture

4. Read the following sentences:

> His leg sustained a fracture.
> The bottle contains a pink mixture.
> A puncture can be dangerous.
> This picture gives me pleasure.

5. Read:

> A picture hangs on the kitchen wall. Peter looks at it when he sits at the table and eats his egg and chips. This picture gives Peter great pleasure.

> The picture glows with brilliant blues and greens. It is a picture of a farm in summer. A tall barn throws a shadow on a blue pool. A few white ducks march in line up a sandy path. A little boy dangles his floppy legs at the edge of the pool and looks up at the fluffy clouds.

> The mood is gentle. The day is still. The sky in the picture is a perfect blue.

❧ LESSON **FIFTY-NINE** ❧

Introduce the consonant sound **f** (as in in **phonics**) and *blend*.

1. **Read, write and practise:**

telephone	telegraph	phrase
photograph	prophet	graphics
elephant	orphan	phonics
alphabet	paragraph	saxophone

2. **Read the following sentences:**

An elephant has a long trunk.
He plays the saxophone well.
The Daily Telegraph is a newspaper.
I like the red telephone on his desk.

Take the family photograph and place it on the shelf.

3. **Read:**

On the shelf next to the fridge in the kitchen is a photograph. It is an old black and white photograph. In it I see my mum and my dad and my big brother Tommy sitting on an elephant. Tommy is now a doctor. In this photograph he is a little boy with a funny face just like me. I am nine. It is a fine photograph. Maybe when I grow up I shall be a doctor too and look back at such photographs.

Introduce some silent letters: **k** (as in **knee**), **w** (as in **wrong**), **b** (as in **lamb**), **h** (as in **school**) and **g** (as in **gnat**). Practise *blending*.

1. **Read, write and practise:**

knee	kneel	knelt
knife	knave	knock
know	knowledge	knit
wrong	wrist	wrap
wrinkle	wreck	write
lamb	limb	dumb
numb	thumb	bomb
crumb	doubt	doubtful
honest	honesty	honour
dishonest	dishonesty	dishonour
school	schooner	scholastic
scholarship	schematic	schism
gnat	gnaw	gnash
gnome	gnarl	gnostic

2. **Read the following sentences:**

Lambs look cute.
John goes to Holland House School.
An honest man is honourable.
Wrap his knee in ice.

You must correct that sum if it is
wrong.
I cannot feel my thumb if it is numb.
You need a strong wrist to write a lot.

When you lay the table put the knife on
the right.

When you have time you can write out
all the sounds you remember.

❧ LESSON **SIXTY-ONE** ❧

Introduce the **kw** sound (as in **quest**) and the capital letter **Q**. Practise *blending*.

[Note: in itself, the **kw** sound cannot be considered one of the 44 sounds since it is a blend of the two sounds ☞ **k** + **w**. However, it is surely most convenient to practise this particular *blending* as one sound denoted by an easily identifiable combination of letters.]

[Spelling rule: the consonant **q** is always followed by the vowel **u**.]

1. **Read, write and practise:**

quest	quell	queen
quick	quickly	question
quit	quite	quiet
quin	squiggle	Quebec
squint	grandiloquent	quote

2. **Read the following sentences:**

It is quite hot under a quilt.
The duck on the pond quacks.
Repeat the question.
The athlete can run quickly.
He emigrated to Quebec in Canada.
You must not squint when you read.
It is quite quiet in the church.
In olden days knights honoured kings and queens.

164

❧ LESSON **SIXTY-TWO** ❧

Introduce the consonant sounds **z** (as in **zoo**) and the capital letter **Z** and *blend*.

1. **Read, write and practise:**

quiz	zebra	zoo
zoom	zenith	wizard
whizz	Zanzibar	zero
zest	zinc	zodiac
zone	New Zealand	zany

2. **Read the following setences:**

In England zebras live in zoos.
This quiz has too many questions.
Add lemon zest to the cake.
Let us whizz off to New Zealand.

Go and see the wizard from Zanzibar.
The zoom lens on the telescope is powerful.

3. **Read and revise:**

Max and Della Bartok lived far away in Zanzibar in a small sugar-pink flat with pink flowers. Della had real flowers in window boxes, paper petals on the pink walls and a white daisy chain

on the green carpet. She had been brought up out of town in a ramshackle bungalow. Flowers grew right up to the window. Sunflowers turned big yellow heads and exchanged flat golden glances with her. Tall red poppies danced in the long untidy grass. Flowers grew all around.

Max Bartok balanced huge spectacles with metal rims on his nose. He was terribly absent-minded. In fact his nose was so long that his spectacles slipped gently along to the tip of it. Then he could not see very well.

Max had been a bad student of law since he would mix all his cases up. His grandfather had been a distinguished and grandiloquent speaker in Parliament and had left Max quite a treasure – a library of miniature old books in a glass case. But Max did not like to work or to read books. He was too lazy. It was much better to eat cakes, doze off and sit in a fluffy pair of slippers.

On a sunny spring day Max decided to do a nice thing for Della who loved flowers. He decided to pick a bunch of flowers for her.

In his hurry and excitement he forgot that his spectacles had slid to the end of his nose.

Instead of picking pink flowers from the window box on the veranda he took all the pink flowers off the lovely wallpaper.

You can imagine how upset Della was when she came out of the kitchen with a big tray of cakes and saw her treasured paper flowers dripping in a flowerpot in the middle of the table. And Max was upset too when he had a good look through his thick spectacles with metal rims.

However he set matters to right when he went to the florist and bought dozens of pink roses. He covered the walls of the room in roses and all was forgiven.

Della and Max continue to live in a sugar-pink flat full of roses in Zanzibar.

Stories to read aloud and enjoy

The Adventures of Ponti Panda

Ponti Panda's
Blue Pants

Ponti Panda decided he was too fat! His best blue pants did not fit over his fat tummy! That was bad, very bad. He loved his blue pants.

He put his furry, black paws over his eyes to shut out the bright sunlight. He had to think. What should he do in order to lose his big fat tummy and wear his best blue pants?

Maybe he should copy the monkeys in the forest and swing from tree to tree. That is called gym. His tummy would surely be trim! Bumping from branch to branch might be fun. No! His panda legs were too short. He would not be able to lose his tummy that way.

Maybe he should stop eating bamboo shoots? Snap, pop, crackle – he just loved bamboo shoots! He rubbed his eyes very hard, extra hard. Bright pink and red spots jumped up and down inside his head. No! He could not stop eating tasty bamboo shoots. Anyway Mummy said bamboo shoots made you grow big and strong. Too big and strong, it seemed!

So much thinking made Ponti Panda rub his black, shiny nose extra hard. He looked around. A green bullfrog rested on a large, round stone a few feet away. "Blup, blip!" went his large full-bellied throat, "Blup, blip!"

Ponti Panda gulped and opened his eyes wide. He stopped thinking hard and stared. His eyes grew as big as two saucepans. Now why can't my tummy go in and out like that? Blup, blip! Blup – out, for large helpings of his crunchy bamboo shoots. Blip – in, for his best blue pants!

Ponti Panda decided to try "blupping" and "blipping".

He lay down on his back. He peered down his nose. Of course, he couldn't see his toes. He shut his eyes tightly and squeezed his tummy in. Tighter, tighter – flatter, flatter – ouff... ouff...!

Then he opened his eyes and looked down. Could he see his toes? No, of course, he couldn't. There was his lovely, round, fat, friendly tummy in its usual place.

"Try harder!" a throaty voice rumbled gently from the round stone a few feet away.

Ponti Panda turned his head to see the big bull-frog blinking his hooded eyelids over his big beacon-eyes.

"Breathe in and count to three. You can count to three, can't you?" added Bullfrog with a chuckle.

"Of course, I can. We learned that at Panda school on our first day. We counted bamboo shoots at lunch time before we ate them."

"You must have learned to count very quickly." Big Bullfrog chuckled so much, his fat chin wobbled like jelly.

Ponti Panda puffed his cheeks out crossly. "You have a very big mouth!" he snapped.

"Come, come! Didn't they teach you good manners?" blupped the Bullfrog. Ponti remembered his very strict teacher, Mrs Mitten. She would not have approved. He sat up and said he was sorry.

"That's better," blipped Bullfrog. "Now, you want to wear your best blue pants, don't you? And they don't fit."

Ponti Panda's ears flopped. His toes curled up. His nose lost its shine and he nodded himself into a sad, soppy lump.

Bullfrog shook his head wisely and stared with interest over Ponti Panda's head at a juicy gnat buzzing lazily in the warm air. Then he said simply, "You need to move the buttons."

Ponti Panda sat up with a jolt. Now why had he not thought of that? What a wally he had been! But he could not sew; his paws were too big. Just as one ear began to flop, wise Bullfrog added, "Woody Woodpecker will snap your buttons off and Sally Spider will spin you a beautiful thread, blue as the sky. That way you can wear your beautiful blue pants and munch bamboo shoots at the same time."

Ponti Panda's cheeks shone pink with delight. "Thank you, thank you," he gurgled as he ran to do what wise Bullfrog had suggested.

Bullfrog blupped and blipped patiently for the gnat to buzz closer. "It won't be quite so easy to give advice next time," he thought as he prepared to snap up his dinner.

Ponti Panda's
First Science Lesson

Ponti Panda lay in his favourite position on his back with his tummy in the air. His legs flopped lazily just like two stuffed sausages.

He was thinking. His eyes were half-closed. Last night he had watched the moon as it travelled gracefully overhead. He had stared closely at the clouds drifting silently over the moon's sad face. Now why did they move so silently and without effort? Cars moved noisily. Aeroplanes flew noisily. Whipping cream for his favourite iced sponge cake made a frightful din. If he discovered how clouds moved silently, then he could invent a silent car, a silent plane, a silent cake mixer. That would be a discovery!

Ponti remained still. His thoughts buzzed. His thoughts were deep.

A plain white butterfly settled on his nose. It tickled. He sneezed. His sneeze was like a strong wind. It blew with such a force that the butterfly was knocked into a rose bush and felt quite giddy.

Ponti was so sorry. He took

out his white hanky and waived it in his friendliest manner so that it looked like another giant, white, friendly butterfly. Only then did he blow his black nose hard. That cleared his head.

He too wished to fly. He could then reach the moon and ask how the clouds went by so silently.

For some months now he had been thinking of making his own flying machine. Now the butterfly had given him an idea. Giant butterfly wings would definitely do the trick.

He rushed to the linen cupboard. Hankies were too small. Sheets were too big. Pillow cases looked just right, especially the ones with pink flowers. He loved pink flowers. His special wings would have pink flowers.

Ponti took two metal hangers out of the cupboard. With lots of huffing and puffing he unwound them and looped two large hoops. He popped one pillow case over the hoop. The pink flowers spread out on the smooth white wing. He did the same again with a second pillow case. Then he rushed out onto the sunny lawn to spread his new wings.

A friendly bee was taken in and landed on a pink flower thinking it was real. "Silly bee," thought Ponti as he gently brushed it aside. With a wing under each arm, Ponti prepared for take-off. "On your marks, get set, go!" he chanted, just like the old sports master. Off Ponti trotted, faster and faster. He finally took a big leap and landed plop in one big heap. He picked himself up. "If you don't succeed, try and try again." The stern voice of Mrs Mitten, the class teacher, drummed in his head. "Take-off two!" Ponti announced loudly.

"Blup! Blip! That will never do!" The voice rolled off big Bullfrog's long tongue as he blinked his wise green eye at Ponti. "You need a tree-top!"

"Why?" quizzed Ponti.

"There's a wind in a tree-top. You must catch the wind," rumbled Bullfrog.

"What a good idea," thought Ponti. He rushed to the largest, fattest, tallest tree in view. Huffing and puffing and tugging his home-made wings, higher and higher he climbed.

From the top he looked down. Green Bullfrog shimmered below, an emerald dot set in a silver pond.

Ponti's heart fluttered like the butterfly wings he had made. They were now a little torn and were missing a few pink flowers. Ponti's toes curled over a rough branch. His tummy button tingled and a breeze tickled his armpit. He spread out his pillow-case wings, swayed for a moment on the topmost branch and jumped.

The air rushed past his flapping ears. His sausage legs bicycled in the air. Like a fat balloon he rocketed this way and that above the pond.

Splash! His hoop wings settled like two white lilies on the water. Ponti climbed out, very limp and wet. He sat on Bullfrog's wet stone.

"So what pushes the clouds by, my flying friend?" chuckled Bullfrog.

Ponti remembered his descent, his ears firing like popcorn. "The air, the air!" he shouted excitedly. "The air! I could not see it, but I could feel it whooshing past my ears. It pushes and shoves this way and that. It pushed the clouds just as it pushed me!"

"Only air between me and the moon," he thought as he lay out to dry in his favourite position on his back, his tummy in the air, his legs like two stuffed sausages flopping lazily.

A butterfly landed on his nose. Ponti Panda decided that next time he wanted to fly to the moon, he would buy a ticket. But he had learned his first science lesson. He had discovered that the air was really there. Not bad for a Ponti Panda.

Ponti Panda
Goes Tap-Dancing

Ponti Panda was day-dreaming. He wanted to be a tap dancer.

He wanted to wear shiny black shoes with shiny toe-taps that jingle-jangled and fired sparks on the floor. He wanted to be in a big show and wear a top hat and a long coat with silver and blue buttons.

Ponti did have a fine pair of black shoes. That was a start. All they needed was a bit of silver tapped onto the toes and another bit of silver tapped onto the heels.

He did have just a few shiny tin coins hidden away in a pink match box. They would be just the right size.

Ponti tumbled out of his bed, landed bump on the fleecy rug and pulled open his big toy box. Four large flat shiny tin coins stared up at Ponti from a bed of soft cotton wool in the pink match box. "Time to

put you to good use," thought Ponti as he took them out and measured them against his fat toes and heel. A perfect fit!

Just how was he going to fix them to his shiny black shoes? String? No! Rubber bands? Definitely not! Sticky sweeties might just work! Gum from a gum tree? No! None of these were strong enough. He would have to use hammer and nails.

Bullfrog would know where to find hammer and nails. He knew everything.

"Blip, blup!" was Bullfrog's greeting as Ponti came tripping along with shoes under one arm and coins jangling in his pocket.

"Try Mr Manners from Down-Under-Farm," blip-blupped Bullfrog in answer to Ponti's question.

"Of course," thought Ponti. Mr Manners used to work in a big factory that made shoes.

Mr Manners was puzzled. He knew all about leather shoes, plastic shoes, rubber shoes, gum shoes, wellies, slippers, trainers, but tap shoes for a fat Ponti Panda! That was new. Hammer and tiny nails he had.

Ponti tripped off with his shoes under one arm, a big hammer under the other and a few tiny nails jingle-jangled in his pocket along with the silvery coins.

"Tapping already," blipped Bullfrog as Ponti tripped past.

Ponti found a big stone slab, balanced his black shoe with one silver piece on top and with a huff and a puff, he tapped out a thumpy tune so that the short little nail fixed his silvery penny beautifully, just where he wanted it. Wonderful!

A few more taps, a few more huffs and a perfect pair of dancing shoes perched proudly on the flat stone slab. Ponti jumped onto it, popped his feet in, clapped his hands and tapped his foot.

Tap, tap,
Jingle, jangle,
Shimmy, shimmy,
Swing!
"Blip, blup," went Bullfrog in time to the tapping.
"Bubble, bubble," went the fish in the pond.
And Ponti danced!

His eyes bobbed up and down. His straw hat popped up and down. His ears grew pink and a few silver buttons flew off his jacket. He forgot that he wanted to be in a show and wear a top hat and a long coat. All he wanted was to dance up and down in the warm sunshine with Blip-blup, his froggy friend, looking on and bubbles floating across the water. Swish, swish, went the fish's tail.

Ponti Panda bobbed up and down, clapped his hands and made such a racket, such a din, that everyone wanted to join in as he

Tap, tapped
Jingle, jangled,
Shimmy, shimmied
And danced!

Ponti Panda
Learns to Paint

Ponti Panda trotted down his favourite path. It was mushy and muddy. His new green boots were just right for this late, very late summer walk.

The sun was low. The clouds were gentle, white and whispy. It was quiet. It was evening.

Ponti stopped and looked across the pond. A birch tree stood very tall. Its bark glittered a brilliant spotty white. Its trunk mirrored a white jagged path across the water to Ponti's feet. It traced a long thin bridge. On each side of the birch-tree bridge, leaves had settled like gold coins on the still dark water.

To one side a fat rowan bush showed off its cluster of brilliant red berries. They reminded him of sweet jelly beans and candy.

Ponti sniffed at the air. He smelt a sour green apple smell – the smell of late summer after a heavy rainfall. Ponti sat down. He saw that the sun had turned the roof of a distant house into an even deeper black.

Ponti liked all this. The setting sun had sharpened the lines and deepened nature's colours. Ponti wanted to keep this picture. He wanted to fix it in his head. Could he not do the same as the setting sun with lines and light and colour? Lines! He could paint lines on paper. He could paint colours on paper. Light and lines and colour make a picture.

Ponti liked the gold coins in the pond. He liked the deep red berries. He wanted to put the red berries onto the white tree trunk to make his very own tree. It would be all white and red. He liked the black roof. He wanted to put gold coins on a black roof.

Ponti shut his eyes. He could do all this. He could do it with paint on paper. It would be fixed forever. And not just the way it was this evening but his way, his own special way. A red and white tree and a black and gold pond – just like great painters did.

A scruffy dog ambled towards him and sniffed one muddy green boot. Ponti could put a dog into the picture too. But in his picture the dog would not be

scruffy. Ponti would give him a brilliant white coat and put a few red dots on his back, a splash of red berries so that everyone could see him better!

The scruffy dog left his boot and scampered off after a duck. The duck was black and grey. Ponti decided a duck would look good in his picture too. But he did not want a black and grey duck. His duck could have a silver head, brilliant jade-green flappy wings and a star on its tail!

That was how to paint it! That was how to paint a real picture, his picture. Ponti took in a sharp excited breath and smelt again the sour air. How could he put that air into the picture? To add a green apple tree was no good. Besides he could not do better than the green apple tree with its knotty bark and curved branches which grew at the end of his garden. Instead of a real tree, he could paint a pale green colour all over his picture – the green smell of apple colour. The picture was clear in his head.

Ponti got up. He waved goodbye to the round evening sun that had deepened nature's colours and given him an idea how to paint. He glowed inside and the sun filled his heart. The sun would have to be in his picture too – both the sun and his heart! But where could he put that sun?

Ponti stopped and dug his green heels into the soft mud. Of course, he would capture the golden sun and pop it at the bottom of the pond. He decided to paint a big yellow blob at the bottom of the pond. Then he could spin golden threads to the coins that he had seen in the dark water and light would glow outwards from inside the picture.

Ponti's heart thumped wildly as the great picture grew in his head. He leapt forward and almost lost his squelchy boots in the soft mud. He was so happy!

Ponti Panda's New Hat

Ben, the butterfly, sat on Bullfrog's head as on a soft green stone. He spread his wings in the warm sunshine and showed off daring colours of green and gold.

Ponti Panda jogged gently by and stopped. He eyed Bullfrog sitting contentedly under the butterfly's shady wings.

"What a smart hat," thought Ponti Panda. "Very smart indeed!"

Last Christmas he had seen lots of hats, red hats with white bobbles. So he knew about woolly hats for snow-time. It was now Easter time – he certainly would not wear an Easter bonnet with ribbons and twirly bits coming down – that was definitely for girls. He had a straw hat for summer time but his straw hat prickled. A hanky on his head was none too smart. Yes, Ponti wanted a hat. He could not sew and he could not knit. How could he make a hat – a proper hat, a smart hat, a hat for the spring sun – a shady sun hat?

Such a sigh escaped from his lips that it gushed right over Bull-frog's head like a big cloud. Ben, the butterfly, snapped his wings shut to escape the sudden draft.

Ponti's eyes popped up. This was even better – a hat that changed shape instead of falling off when the wind blew. Just what he wanted. Why didn't such a dream hat float down from the sky like a flying saucer? He could then pop it on his head. Yes, he wished he could have a large, flat, green and gold sun hat.

Ponti sat down on his favourite stone slab and dabbled his toes in the pond; first his big toe, then his little toe and then all the ones in between.

Sounds of laughter rippled across the green grassy hill. Children were playing a jolly game of football or catch-ball or run-and-jump. Ponti wanted to know just what it was they were throwing. It kept landing plop on the grass. It certainly wasn't a bouncy ball. The thick hedge was far too high for him. Ponti stared up into the sky wondering woefully. He had even lost his thinking cap! Certainly, his thinking cap was in a huff because Ponti was dreaming about another sort of hat!

For the second time that day Ponti's eyes popped up. Circling out of the blue in a wide sweep, a flying saucer traced a wide and beautiful arc, bumped along the grassy bank and landed right at Ponti's feet. It was flat. It was green. It was round. It would make a perfect hat. In fact, it was a frisbee made of the lightest green plastic and curved to catch the wind.

Ponti bent down, lifted the flat, green saucer, examined it carefully and popped it on his head. He looked at himself in the water. Very smart indeed! What a beautiful sun hat!

Ponti sauntered along with a saucy smile on his face. Ben, the butterfly, fluttered his wings and floated into the air.

He had spied Ponti's new hat. It looked to him just like a lovely large round green leaf. Ben, the butterfly, landed gently on Ponti's round flat green head and folded his wings.

Ponti was not past admiring himself again, so he turned and looked at his reflection in the clean pond water. He saw his new hat. Better than ever! For perched between his ears was cheeky Ben. Cheeky Ben had added his magical touch atop Ponti's head. The jaunty slant of a butterfly's wings rippled over the water.

A Bit of Butterfly
A Short Story

Zanda felt very tired. He had been old for many years now and when he felt tired he felt very sad. Perhaps he felt sad first and tired afterwards.

It was mid-winter. It was cold, very cold. He had been working on his history manuscript for far too long. He had not lit his fire once this winter, so absorbed had he been by his work. That was not right. It was time to rest. He dimmed his lamp, lit his gas heater and went to an old comfortable leather chair torn at the armrests. He sat back. The gas spluttered and awoke after its long hibernation. The room took on a warm glow.

For many years Zanda had been a bit of a crotchety fellow. You see he had left the world a long time ago. He had stopped living with people and half a century is a very long time if you live all alone.

Zanda has spent his life writing up the history of mankind, a history against the cruelty of mankind. He had then written to people and read about life in the world. He did not like what people said at all. It sounded just as he had imagined in his own book. In fact it sounded very bad. So he had to rewrite his book in even blacker colours. He had done this several times so you can imagine just how gloomy his book was.

Something stirred on the mantelshelf – a sleepy butterfly. Zanda would never have spotted it but for a spurt of the gas fire.

Zanda knew it was a custom to kill butterflies – catch them in butterfly nets and pin them in glass cases in neat rows. Zanda refused to kill a living thing so he let it be. Besides it was difficult for him to move at present. He felt so old and cold.

It occurred to him that perhaps it was time for him to die and he wondered whether others would read his work. He remembered that a clever young man was supposed to be visiting him soon. Yes, he must tell the young man about life.

Zanda sat very still. The butterfly unstuck its wings and threw dust in all directions. Dust reached his nose. He awoke. He found himself looking at a butterfly, dust-free and in all its glory. It was a brilliant yellow, so transparent that the light caught its bright green spots. The old man had never before seen such a lovely object. Or had he? Yes, long ago. The yellow reminded him of pale winter sun on snow. The green on the wings reminded him of a walk in a dark green pine forest long ago and the dancing sunlight in the trees. He sat entranced for many moments.

Then he remembered his work – his great work for posterity. How could he leave such a vision of doom and gloom? He took his melancholy manuscript and burned it. Then he sat down and began to work again. The butterfly followed the daily scratching of the pen.

It fluttered and rainbowed its colours over the face of the old man.

Zanda finished his book. He laid down his pen. His history of the world was cruel indeed but he had added one chapter about a butterfly. To this chapter he gave his greatest attention. Then he found an old paint box and stirred up wonderful colours. He illustrated his last chapter as the sages of old did. He was happy. When his work was finished he laid down his pen and slept. Then he died very gently of old age.

It is well known that a butterfly will not live long. It too was content to sink gently down on the neatly written manuscript.

The clever young man came to visit. He read the work and marvelled at the last chapter for he was young and in love with life. He took the work into the world. It was read and the old man became famous. And it was all on account of a butterfly.